"Butterflies can't see their wings.

They can't see how truly beautiful they are,

but everyone else can.

People are like that as well."

- Anonymous

The Butterfly Letters—Book One

Compilation & Commentary by Elijah Kihlstadius

Transcribed & Edited by Lauren Kibler

Elijah Kihlstadius
PO Box 1211
Burnsville, MN 55337
United States
www.justaskinnyboy.com

More information at:
www.butterflyletters.org

ISBN-10: 1494289563
ISBN-13: 978-1494289560

Printed in the United States of America

First Edition: January 2014
10 9 8 7 6 5 4 3 2 1

Butterfly Letters is a division of the Life & Love organization
www.findlifeandlove.org

The Butterfly Letters

Book One

Compilation & Commentary by
Elijah Kihlstadius

Transcribed & Edited by
Lauren Kibler

This book is dedicated to Jacklyn,
may her story never fall on deaf ears again.

Acknowledgements

My other half, Lauren Kibler, the girl who gave me the courage and motivation to turn this idea into a reality. I couldn't have done it without you. Thanks for always being the best thing that's ever happened to me.

My radiant friend, Amada Stapp, for encouraging me when I need it most; your light is a constant reminder of what grace and love can really do. Thank you for giving me my life back.

My dear friend, Holly Graffunder, who has always been one of the wisest and most kind hearted girls I've ever known. Thank you for always helping me keep my feet on the ground and my head out of the clouds. Also, for convincing me that no one could ever love horses as much as she does. I'm proud to call her my friend.

My crazy family, who has always been there for me when I need them most. You guys sure drive me nuts sometimes, but boy do I love you, and God only knows what I would do without you all. I'm honored to be a part of the Kihlstadius Klan.

My Mother and Father, for raising me up to become who I am today and for always trying your best to do what is right for me even during the times when I didn't want you to or wouldn't accept it. You are literally the reason for why I am who I am and why I will be what I become. Thank you for putting up with me.

My ~~fans, followers, and subscribers~~ **friends** who have always been there for me and have given me the confidence to express myself through my blog and my YouTube videos. Thank you for everything; I wouldn't be where I am today if it wasn't for you.

My Lord and savior Jesus Christ, the reason I now know the priceless value of the human soul and what it means to be truly and wholly loved.

Disclaimer:

This publication is designed to provide accurate and personal experience information in regards to the subject matter covered. It is sold with the understanding that the author and contributors are not engaged in rendering counseling or other professional services. If counseling advice or other expert assistance is required, the services of a professional should be sought out.

Every letter whose author was known is used with permission from the writer. Many of the letters wished to remain anonymous or not have their identity known beyond their first name and thus we have removed all information from the letters that might indicate the writers' identity. For example, all surnames have been removed from the pictures and not included in the text.

Any person who sends or has sent mail to Butterfly Letters is agreeing* to the following terms:

1. Confirmation of Understanding of Consent

I hereby confirm that I have sent a letter to Elijah Kihlstadius (hereafter referred to as the RECIPIENT) with respect to a book for general publication which he is writing. I confirm that the RECIPIENT explained to me at the outset that some or all of what I wrote in my letter, with the exception of any details in relation to my identity, might appear in the book but that in no event would my words be taken out of context. I understand that my statements may form the basis for conclusions and discussions of issues relating to the book's general subject. I also realize that the RECIPIENT may transfer ownership of his/her work or may authorize others to publish material and that it may appear in magazines, other articles, treatises, collections, subsequent editions, and other written forms as well as in electronic, audio, or audiovisual presentations including educational and commercial television programs and movies.

2. Confirmation of Voluntariness

I confirm that I have voluntarily disclosed to the RECIPIENT information and opinions about myself and other individuals.

3. Confirmation of Reliance

I understand that the RECIPIENT will expend extensive and valuable time and effort in preparing a manuscript based on the content of my letter and has relied on my consent to use this material.

4. Consent to Use Material and Name

I hereby consent to all publication of any or all of the material disclosed by me within the letter and to identify me as its subject or source and to the use of my name (and likeness) in the published material and in any promotion or advertising of it.

5. Confirmation to rescind any rights to compensation

I rescind my right to compensation or royalties and confirm that the RECIPIENT will not be obligated to provide compensation or royalties in any form, be it monetary or otherwise specified.

*— Terms are open to discussion should any concerns or disputes arise and may be modified upon request.

Table of Contents

Foreword: How it all started

My name is Elijah Kihlstadius. At the time of writing this, I am twenty one years old and I live in St. Paul, Minnesota. I'd like to give you some of my story and the story behind this project in order to help you build some context for the rest of the book.

Let's rewind the calendar back to February of 2011 and start from there. Up until this point, I had been struggling and hurting, but had no intentions of doing anything about it. But what happened this month changed all of that. That month I decided that it was time for me to recover (whatever that meant). As part of that step, I started a blog on a website called tumblr.

This blog, started on March 1st 2011, would become a huge catalyst for some of the biggest changes in my life. It allowed me to connect with other people who were going through the same things I dealt with on a daily basis, and it gave me a place where I didn't have to be alone in my struggles.

Of course, I started this blog for me. I wanted to record my story, to keep track of where I had been so that someday, later on down the road, I could look back and say "hey, that's where I was. But I made it through it, so you can too!" That was what I wanted, that was what I expected.

What I did not expect, however, was the response I got from people reading my story and my blog. I began to receive dozens–if not hundreds–of messages from other people online telling me how 'inspiring' I was. People would often tell me how they had not met a guy who was so open about his struggles. There were even a few people who, through some simple reaching out and listening, told me that I had saved their life because I gave them hope when they needed it most.

Needless to say, I realized very quickly that what I was doing with this little blog of mine was much bigger than me. I knew that this was a huge opportunity, and it was an opportunity that I wasn't going to waste. It didn't seem like something I knew how to do, but I tried anyway because I knew that there were people out there that didn't have someone to go to. I knew that there were lots of people out there who were just like me; scared, hurting, and alone.

A little over a year later in May 2012, I registered for a PO box at my local post office. At the time I simply did it because I wanted to ask people if they would send me letters and cards for my birthday. But again, this turned out to be much bigger than I expected.

See, this is where the letters and stories come in. After my birthday had come and gone, people still wanted to send me letters. I gladly accepted, and because of how positive the response was I even encouraged people to send me letters. I began to receive letters quite regularly, and after a few months I had so many letters that I had to buy a large scrapbook just so I could keep them all organized.

Of course, it wasn't only letters that I received. Many people sent me drawings, pictures, cards, and other fun things. But the most personal and real things that I got were the letters, many of which were stories that I knew no one had read or heard before. It was both heartbreaking and encouraging to read so many stories from these individuals whom, though I had never been introduced to, I felt like I now knew personally.

By the end of 2012, I had well over 100 letters. In early January, 2013 I decided that I wanted to find a way to share those letters and stories with the world. That was when I began developing the idea of putting my letters into a book. It started as a very small and very simple concept, but like many of my ideas in the past, it quickly became much bigger than just me and I realized how important my message really was.

This book is 25 letters that have been hand picked out of the 200+ letters in my scrapbook. 25 stories from 25 people. I hope they touch your heart as much as they've touched mine.

How the book works

What's Inside:

This book is composed of many stories, ranging from short to long, tragic to cheerful, light hearted to heartbreaking. While these letters are grouped together in this book intentionally, it is important to remember that each letter is its own individual story, belonging to an individual person. As such, I highly encourage you to read each chapter void of comparison to any other chapter.

I also encourage you to bear in mind that these letters are by no means literary masterpieces. They are personal, raw, and organic. Read them through the eyes of one who has just received that letter and is eager to know the message it contains.

There will be strong and graphic content in some of these letters. Topics such as self harm, suicide, eating disorders, and abuse are mentioned in multiple chapters. Each chapter will give trigger warnings that will indicate what topics are mentioned in that particular chapter.

Please do your best to understand them from the perspective of the writer, as doing so will help you get a better view of how that particular thing affects their life as a whole.

If there is a portion or page of a letter that is illegible, you may find a transcribed version of that letter in the back of the book. For an index of transcriptions, go to page 170

If you are interested in reading a letter that mentions a specific topic, there is an index of topics on page 228.

Make It Yours:

This book isn't just mine. It's *yours*. Mark it as you will, friend. Whether that's marks of tears, or fresh highlighter, or simply the corner of your favorite page turned down, make this book yours. Let it hit you. Let your heart concern itself with the memories resurfacing as your eyes take in these stories. Write your thoughts, circle your favorite words, sentences, or paragraphs. Make it personal. Because it is personal. This is for you.

You are welcome here.

Part One

~

The Letters

What is a butterfly letter?

The term "butterfly letter" used for the title of the book comes from the quote which is printed at the front of this book.

"Butterflies can't see their wings. They can't see how truly beautiful they are, but everyone else can. People are like that as well."

- Anonymous

Everyone's story is like the wings of a butterfly. We can't always see how special or important our own story really is. We can't help it, it's just our life; it's what we've always known. But if we look at someone *else's* life and story, then we can clearly see how beautiful their story really is.

This idea first came to me when I started receiving letters in the mail and I started to realize how most, if not all, of the people who had sent me letters had no idea how incredible their story really was. I began to wonder if everyone felt like that; if everyone thought that their story wasn't beautiful because they couldn't see it from the outside. It even dawned on me that I myself had not considered my own story to be one of great value.

It was through those letters that I started to look at people and their stories in a whole different light. Those letters and the hearts behind them gave me a passion for showing people that stories–especially their own stories–are incredibly valuable and should never be taken for granted. I fell in love with the power of a person's story, and I finally grasped just how exceptionally beautiful stories are.

The Butterfly Letters is a book series that I am starting because I believe that these simple letters– these basic and sometimes messy letters– have a kind of realness and intimacy that no amount of fiction writing can amount to. Because these letters are real. Their writers are real. The stories are real. And they are **beautiful.**

Chapter One
Jacklyn

Trigger Warning: Suicide, Eating Disorders, Self Harm, Abuse

Transcription on page 171

The Butterfly Letters is dedicated to Jacklyn.

Jacklyn and I started talking in May of 2012 through an anonymous chat feature that I put on my tumblr. Over the next month we had many conversations via this chat feature, but one night in the middle of June, things were worse than usual. She was struggling greatly, and I was exhausted from typing, so I invited her onto a chatroom website so I could talk (via voice chat) and she could still type. I had talked with many people who were struggling, but for some reason, it was different this time. Jacklyn was different. I could see this immense darkness and brokenness that was completely suffocating her. It broke my heart, and I knew that she needed to know that she was worth it.

During that conversation I asked her to mail me the blade that she used to harm herself. She agreed, and that is where the first letter came from. A short time later, we were messaging again and she told me that she wasn't going to be bothering me anymore after July 1st. Naturally this concerned me, so I begged her not to leave because I knew what she was implying.

Remember though, that the whole time she remained anonymous whenever we conversed. She would only identify herself by saying "This is Jacklyn," so I had no way of contacting her or finding out what might have happened to her. I just had to wait and hope to hear from her again.

Much to my relief I received a second letter from her on July 5th. In this letter, she admitted that she had gotten two more blades (which she sent with the letter) and also that she had been planning to kill herself on July 1st, which is why she had said that I wouldn't be bothered by her anymore. But more importantly, she also wrote that, because I insisted she stay, she promised she would give life a second chance; she included her suicide note (see page 20) as a sign of her choice.

In the following months Jacklyn and I still talked off and on through Facebook and Twitter instead of the anonymous messaging. She still struggled a lot and she still had that darkness and brokenness about her, but I could see that it was beginning to lessen.

She wrote to me again in September, only this time she chose to share her story with me. It was at this point that I realized just how honored I was. Not only had this girl confessed her brokenness to me, but she also trusted me with this precious story about her life. I knew then that what I was doing by reaching out to people was not only important, but it was powerful and life changing to those that I had the honor of impacting. I learned all of this thanks to a broken and beautiful girl named Jacklyn.

So why am I dedicating the book to her?

Well, I have two reasons:

First, because when I opened the letter and read what she had said about her suicide note, I made a promise then and there both to her and to myself that I would share her story.

Second, simply put, Jacklyn has changed *my* life in a way that I cannot thank her enough for. It is because of her that I understand the value of taking the time simply to listen. This is the least I can do to repay her.

Thank you, Jacklyn. I hope you enjoy this book; I couldn't have done it without you.

June 21, 2012

Dear Elijah,

Thank You! Thank you so so so much. Really thank you because of what you did last night, you didnt have to but you did, so thank you. Last night you made me realize something You made me realize that if I really try hard enough I dont need to cut I now know that

So you are probably wondering who this is, unless you figured it out already because you are super smart. It is like 3am and I'll probably go run in an hour or so, but I would figure you know now. Well I figured maybe I would, right now, say thank you & tell you how much last night meant. I know you wont say it but I know you would have much rather have talked to Danielle than me last night or slept or done something much more productive than talk to me so thank you. It is greatly appreciated that someone in Minnesotta cares about someone so insignificant like me. So thank you.

Eventually I'll mail you the blade I will try. I dont really know cause I am extremly dependent on it, but I'll try everyday this summer if I make it through to send you it. I promise, scratch that pinky promise. I'm going to force myself now to when I walk to the mailbox to send this but... we will see what happens.

I hope to make you happy. Take care of yourself

Love,

Jacklyn

July 8, 2012

Dear Elijah,

Thank YOU for everything! Really it means so much to me, you dont even know. Seriously, I think, well actually know, you are the first person to really care in a long time. That means a lot because you don't even know me but are willing to do that. So THANK YOU

I am sending you my last two blades[1]. I promise they are my last two. I promise you that I will try and stay clean and safe. I promise you I will try not to self harm anymore because it means so much to you. So if that is what makes you happy and will make you keep helping people than it is truely worth it. I just want to say: You were right. You were right when you said I couldnt controll it. You were and I am sorry I didnt listen.

I dont know how much the next page is going to mean to you. But let me explain something. Remember when I said starting July I would never bother you again? well... I planned something. I couldn't tell you. Why? Either:

ⓐ you would be crushed and blame yourself

ⓑ you would have tried to talk me away from it

ⓒ a mix of both a & b.

So I am sorry. I never did what I planned. I mean yes Saturday night I cut but I stopped myself from going to far. But their is one thing I learned from your story. That is: If Elijah can make it than so can I so thank you for that. Elijah, I am giving you the note to show you how much I am going to try Okay?

Seriously, You are such an amazing person

[1] To see an image of the blades mentioned in this letter, please see pg. 161

whoever finds this or me I am sorry but this had to be done. The constant bullying inside of school, outside of school, online it was everywhere. But the thing that drove me to this was my best friend telling me to kill myself. So you know what she said that along with others who told me they'd help so you know what no one will notice or care. So I am sorry to whoever finds this. Dont feel bad nor feel like its your fault. Please dont follow. YOU are so important.

I love you.

Jaeklyn.

September 2, 2012

Elijah,

This is probably one of the hardest things I will ever have to write. It shouldn't be but it is and I really wish it wasn't. I cannot promise that this letter will be entirely good, bad, happy, sad, etc. because it is a mix of many emotions. I think after a few scraps of letters on loose leaf I realized I should type it, so I don't kill any more trees! I finally know exactly how I need to get across my message and I also think that I am writing this just because I want someone who I trust to know these things because honestly it isn't getting anywhere.

Anyways do you mind if I tell you a little story? So you can get why I am feeling the way I am. If you don't want to hear this story you don't have to you can just skip down to the exclamation point in the beginning of the paragraph. Okay so here it goes the story. There was this girl, her name was Jackie. Jackie was the girl who wanted to be friends with everyone even if they were the meanest people; she wanted and was their friend. Anyways, as Jackie went into kindergarten she began getting nicknames and being teased for many things. Well it's just kids being kids right? WRONG. Jackie went on to first grade. New school = new friends. She immediately became friends with Debra. Well Debra and her friends immediately clicked with Jackie. But the bullying began. She would be teased for everything. Her weight, the way she wore her hair, because she danced, anything and everything. Well it continued but eventually fifth grade came. Jackie's dad died suddenly. Jackie's school called all the parents in her grade so all the kids knew. They were all her friend. They all went to the wake and the funeral and were her friends for now. But a month later, guess what happened? She was being bullied even worse. That summer she got "tripped" to see her fall. She ended up spraining her knee, breaking her wrist and three fingers, chipping her tooth, and breaking her nose. Just to see her fall. Sixth grade they all apologized but the thing is they apologized because Jackie went to the school psychologist weekly to get over her dad and her sixth grade teacher told her that bullying was going on but he needed her to intervene with him. So she did. Problem fixed right? WRONG. Seventh grade = new school = no problems. WRONG. Shoes thrown off the bus, books thrown out the window, cupcakes thrown at her, being dragged on the bus floor by her backpack. It settled down. Freshman year death threats started and that's when I stopped eating and started burning. I stopped my best friend wanted to kill me for it. So anyways her bra got unhooked in homeroom, her desk flipped, hair was cut, and she got stabbed with a compass (thing for drawing circles). Sophomore year was same thing. Junior year within the first month of school she was told to kill herself, that they would help her kill herself, she was a slut, whore, bitch, whale, she was told in front of the whole cafeteria that an 8th grader would bang her on the bus and many other things. Well her friend Sam found out. She made her tell someone and it "stopped". December came around. She was being told she was a home wrecker, suicidal, personally killing herself and starving herself. Then in February she was grabbed and bled by a guy who was her "friend", the same guy saying those things. She told the dean well he lied. He was supposed to get suspended he got out of it. But it didn't stop there. The last day of school Jackie checked the review group to wish all a happy summer. Someone posted crap about her friend Sam. She immediately went to stick up for her. It ended on Jackie though. It ended with "Jackie if you really want to get serious why don't you get your fat ass off Facebook and hit the elliptical". That drove Jackie to cutting. That also drove her to restricting.

! Nice story right? That Jackie is me. I am so scared to start school on Tuesday you don't understand. If it happens again this year I can't even imagine what will happen. I can't and the thing is the suspension from the kids on the bus was only for junior year that means... they can be on the bus this year. I can't deal with this but I made a promise to myself. If it happens, I tell NO ONE. Why? I don't want to be seen as the problem girl. I can't.

I am sorry lately for cutting. I am sorry for being the fuck up. I am sorry. Lately it's too much. I need help. I know that but the thing is I am scared to ask for it. I know I said I would tell a counselor but... I cant he already thinks I am unable to handle stuff from junior year I can't let him know I am doing this I look up to him I cant. I wish I could though. I wish I wasn't such a chicken. I feel like I might take my life.

I know I should send you my blades again and I know that you will probably tell me to but I can't and there is a good reason behind it. I feel like I put the pressure on myself to quit. I mess up under pressure. Then I get mad at myself because I feel like I made empty promises to you when I sent them because I just fail constantly. Like, I promised but then cut and mess up and become a liar and that hurts because I don't want you to feel that from anyone especially me because I know how much it hurts.

I don't know I just wish my life was worse so that I actually had a reason for being depressed and not just am depressed. I just wish I had a plausible reason to cut. I feel like I don't. I feel like hating me isn't a good enough reason. I feel like being overwhelmed isn't a good enough reason. I just wish I had a better reason to justify it all but I don't and that's the thing no one would believe the "happy" girl does this. They would think it's some crazy messed up joke. I just wish it was. I wish it was a joke and not reality. I wish this wasn't what I got myself into.

My mom doesn't know that since I have been driving with my license that as soon as she lets me on my own I don't think I can because I know one day something will happen and that I will get too upset and that I will just push myself over the edge and I will kill myself with success.

I feel myself pushing away my friends and it scares me. I have isolated and I am scared that I am seeing the signs of me being so close to suicide. I really am scared but then again I think it is better. I am out of everyone's way of life. Everyone can be much happier. I mean at the beginning no but later on yes.

Like tonight I was given the ultimatum by a friend to choose if I want the friendship or if I want it to be done. All because I distanced. It's not fair. I wish he could see how much I am struggling but he wouldn't even understand if anyone tried telling him. So now I can't really push him away when I am overwhelmed because he will end the friendship and I hate that because I know if I don't keep reminding myself not to no matter how scared and overwhelmed I get, I can't because I will lose him.

I don't know I just figured someone should know. Instead of me keeping it all bottled inside. Anyways, take care of yourself. Congrats on your relationship. I wish you well. Remember I love and care about you.

Sorry,

Jaclyn

P.S. When I finish something I am going to have to email it to you because I think you deserve to read it ☺

Chapter Two
"A."

Trigger Warning: Eating Disorders

Transcription on page 176

I hope you can help me. I am not anorexic or bulimic (although my sister an ex both suffered from anorexia). I have never cut into my body. All of my scars are from surgery. Here's the kicker, though: I believe myself to have Dissociative Identity Disorder, with a current total of 15 different identities, or "alters". I am currently seeking diagnosis, but have encountered reluctance from multiple therapists since I appear to function so well in daily life. I am reaching out to you because I need someone to talk to. You seem like such a wise, kind and caring soul, I couldn't not reach out to you. Yesterday in therapy, I asked my therapist if I could let my alters out, in therapy. She discouraged me; said it would be "a step backwards". I was hurt, discouraged that she would advise <u>against</u> expressing myself. All the parts inside me need to be recognized, and cared for. I was hoping the alters that wanted to could write to you, Elijah.

I wish I could include my tools for self-injury, but my most dangerous tool is the self-hate I carry inside myself.

I only included my first initial on the envelope, because I have a unique name and do not wish for my identity to be revealed publicly

I hate being fat. I wish I was thin. I wish I had a gap between my thighs, not just because of the way it looks, but because of the way it feels. I can't wear skirts because I get a painful rash between my thighs. I am hot all the time, and I sweat after minimal exertion. I am 20 years old, but I have to wear granny bras because they don't make cute bras in my size. I can't run.

I wish I was thin so I could fit clothes from forever 21. I wish I was thin so I will be respected. I wish I was thin, so I don't have to be one of the "fat girls". I wish I was thin so my mom would stop making comments on what I eat. I wish I was thin so I could curl up into a tiny fetal ball and hide. I wish I was thin so I could run fast, and far.

It makes me so sad to hate my body; my perfectly functioning body. my body that has kept me alive all these years, and done me no wrong. my body that has survived surgery, meningitis and a car accident. It's not my body's fault, it's mine. I let this happen, and I don't know how to undo it. I don't even know where to start.

Please help,

– Rinala

Chapter Three
Alice

Trigger Warning: Self Harm
Transcription on page 177

Dear Elijah,

I've never written to someone I don't know and have never met. And honestly I'm not really sure what to say. But I've rewritten this letter 3 times wanting it to look perfect, but I realize it's not going to be perfect. Nothing is but that doesn't mean it's terrible.

I first found out about you, was by my friend. I was on tumblr and I saw what my friend wrote about you it was "Also, a person who inspired me is Elijah, I'm sending him my blades and my story on monday." I asked her who you were and went to your tumblr page. I read your story and thought it was incredible and the first video I watched was the one with you and Lauren about your favorite memories and it was your 2 month anniversery. It was the cutest thing ever. Then my friend sent me the one on self harming and it brought me to tears. I loved it. Video's like those, I've never cried when I watched them.

That video was amazing and it touched me. It was amazing for someone to say something that I feel so much of the time. You and Lauren said all the things I'm scared to say to anyone else but inside I'm screaming it silently. I loved feeling not alone.

knowing someone understand's and my favorite thing you two said was "things will get better. It can get better, it does get better. Maybe not tomorrow, maybe not next week, maybe not for a year, but things will get better." Because anytime someone has said that to me or said "it will be okay" I've never fully believed them 100%. But those 3 sentences made me believe 100%.

There's times when I've been at my total worst and have cried out for help silently but have been terrified of the outcome and result. I see that I really am not alone, there are others that are the same as me.

I was going to cut tonight but I didn't and it's thanks to you, Lauren, and my friend. Thank you for saving me tonight, there will probably be more to come but I'll just watch the video and know I'm not alone. Sadly, I'm not strong enough for you're challenge - to send you my blades but I can part with them ~~tonight~~ and that they'll be nowhere near my skin to make a mark. I want to get better and this seems to be a first good small step. Thank you again, so much.

—Alice

Chapter Four
Ana Beatrice

Transcription on page 178

Rio de janeiro, 13 de maio de 2012.
May, 13th 2012.

Hey,

It's 5:30 a.m. on a sunday and I didn't sleep at all. I'm writing you a letter, don't know why but I'm doing anyway. Maybe I want to have one of those friendships by letter that people used to have, but I think that on these letters the person talked about their lives and I'm not gonna do that, That's not my type of letter. Truth to be told I don't really have a type of letter, besides maybe debts. I really don't know what type of letter is that, but probably not a "fan" mail either, 'cause I'm not gonna say how amazing you and your blog are, you already knows that (If you don't I'm opening an exception in these parentheses: You are fucking amazing, you're handsome, smart, artistic, have the perfect eyes, a curly golden hair which is the cutest thing I ever saw and the most important you're trying to help the others. You're like the guy of my dreams, if you want to marry just call me I'm free anytime lol), anyways I really don't know what this letter is about, maybe it is just some random babbling of a insomniac girl. Anothe thing I'm really sorry about my grammar mistakes, I checked this a couple of times but you know, there's always something that slips away.

The envelope contains some others stuff, cause when I wrote this on sunday I wrote it a short story, actually I wrote the story first and I thought about sending you a photo too. Then I got carried away during the week and end up doing a draw and buying some bracelets to you. So I'm gonna tell you about the stuff that I'm sending you. The short story that I wrote It is in portuguese, and I really think it's better this way. I actually write most of my stories in english but for some reason this one came to me in portuguese. So I propose you that it stay that way, that you don't try to translate on dols online translators, 'cause let's be honest my story it's not that good and probably gonna get a lot worse if translated on those. But if you know someone that knows portuguese than that person can translate to you. So it's a deal? Okay, I know you cannot really answer that and you can do whatever you want with the story but I really do hope that you do as I'm asking. One other thing about the short, please take good care of her, it is the only copy that I have and you know may be someday when I'm gonna be like oprah famous you can sell that on ebay :)

I'm sending you a photo which is a monument somewhat famous, the Christ. Okay I know my photo is not wonderful or anything and the quality is pretty bad but I'm not asking you to review or anything and I like this photo a lot. It was taken about a month ago and I really feel like sending to you so you can get to know a bit more abou Rio de janeiro, 'cause I really love this city. And I really want everybody to love too, 'cause my city is wonderful, so beautiful, and I feel like sometimes people let pass it by. There's so much beauty, wonderful places that are not touristics spots and people that live in the city don't really care about or don't see the beauty. Anyways you should come visit something, I would love to welcome you here. Now, about the draw, I did that inspired on the Coldplay song Fix you, which I'm kind obsessed for the past three months, I like a lot the original but I trully love the Boyce Avenue version (they made a cover of What makes you beautiful - One direction and it's amazing, and I'm not really fangirl of OD, okay I am, but there's bits there's not how to not love them). So that's about it of the draw, I really appreciate drawing but I'm not really talented so I guess my art is naif :) Okay not really, on high school I was forced to study technical draw, so I now a bit abou perspective, and unfortunatelly a lot about hospital sectors, so if you need to organize a floorplan of a hospital according to the sector. I'm here for you :) Okay, last but not least there are the 6 racolts, so they come with some words in portuguese, they had wrote in english but I thought portuguese would be cuter. So let me tell you the meanings of the world. Amor = love; Sorriso = smile; Felicidade = happiness; Esperança = hope; Don't worry I'm not fooling about the meaning, you can checke it on google. Oh, If you I can teach you how to say the words :)

So right now it's about 6:30 a.m and soon the people will be celebrating mother's day and the only thing I can think is about the people who don't have what to celebrate or how to celebrate. I really would like to think that today all the people are happy but I know the world doesn't work like that. That our society make lots of peoples cry from sadness, from hungry, from pain, from exploration. There a numerous of people miserable physically, mentally, and you and I know what it's like to suffer and be mentally miserable. You know I really try to help the others, I do think this is my obligation as a citizen, I work voluntarily with the kids, and I really try to treat everyone with respect, as equal. 'Cause after all we are equals independent of ou social status, money or appearance. But I just feel like it what I do is nothing compared to the grand picture, I feel really powerless. I'm a communist, more like a marxist and I really try to fight for equality, fight politically (Before you get scared I'm must say relax, I don't eat children, at least not everyday, they are really hard to cook LOL), but I just feel like it's nothing sometimes. I really like children I always bonded with them and I dream of adopting since I was 10 or 11, and it really brakes my heart that some kids don't have parents, don't have a home, are being abused and we act like it's not our problem. I just ask myself If I'm not part of these childrens problems, I close my eyes for these children like most of us. I just wish I was zillionare and could take and the children that are hurt, that cry. I really think it would be better if I was feeling their pain, and they were happy.

Okay I wrote more that I planned about this. I can't help it, I just got carried away. I just think that we as collectivity should stand up, 'cause we don't have to be always like that, we can be a better society. Society its this way 'cause we build this way, we can rebuild as our wish. We don't have to be oppressed, We don't have to deal with the crap that other people put us through, we can stand up, we can occupy. And I guess in a way it's what you are doing with your blog, you are telling people to not be slaves of others, of their sickness, that we can help each other overcome our illness, , that mental illness lots of times is overlooked and it is as serious as any disease. I trully admire your blog. Once again I got a bit carried away, it's a normal thing for me but usually I'm speaking not writing. I'm aquarius so it's normal. Anyways don't know if you believe in astrology. I sort of do and sort of don't, I try to be open minded but sometimes astrology tell some nonsense.

Ahn I'm sorry that I wrote so much and the end is a bit messy. I like to say thank you if you actually had the patience to read the whole letter, 'cause I know some parts are pretty boring, but anyways most of the letter I wrote without haven't slept at all so I guess I have an excuse. Hope you likes the letter. Any questions about my caligraphy can be on facebook LOL.

Oh, I realize that I didn't say my name or anything. I'm Ana Beatrice, 18 years old, Rio de Janeiro Brasil and that's it I think

Bye sweetie.

P.S.: I decided to send you a postcard of Frankestein, I really like the book, and I love the movie. Old horror movies are always so good to show the sadness of an outsider, a "monster", anyways I took this out of my wall and I'm sending, hope you like it. x.o

Chapter Five
Anna

Trigger Warning: Self Harm

Transcription on page 181

Here Are my Blades[2], All of them.
It's time to recover.
I can do this. I will do this.
For my daughter and, soon to be Here, Son♡
Thanks For the Hope

xo xo,
Anna ♡

P.S.: I wrapped them in tape for saftey ♡

[2] To see an image of the blades mentioned in this letter, please see pg. 161

Chapter Six
Courtney

Trigger Warning: Self Harm

Transcription on page 182

Dear Elijah,

Whenever I get mail it makes me feel happy and loved which is why I decided to send you some. You've made a difference in the world, don't ever forget it. I hope to meet you someday because you're such a sweet and understanding guy and that shows through your videos and blogs.

I wanted to share some of my story with you. A year ago I started my first year of college. I was my first time leaving Delaware and being far away from my family. When I'm at school I only see my family every month or two.

I'm usually a shy person but I tried to be more friendly last year. I tried to be friends with lots of different people but nobody liked me. Even my roomate moved in with someone else leaving me in a dorm by myself. I felt so alone. In addition to that my grades weren't good and I didn't make the colorguard team. All of these things seemed to send me the message "you're not good enough" and "you don't deserve to be happy". My cutting got worse, especially when I tried going to the counseling office. It just made things so much worse. I thought that I couldn't get better on my own but maybe I can.

I'm now starting my second year in college and I hope that this one will be better than the first. I made one really close friend last year and we're rooming together. I joined a club with nice people and now I have someone to eat dinner with every night. I have a chance to fix my GPA so I can stay in the elementary education program.

I want to recover so I'm giving you one of my razor blades. I hope I will give you my other one someday. I've been a month without cutting which probably doesn't sound like much but it's a big deal for me. It's a start. Even though It's been hard it's been worth it. I've been using a lot of distraction techniques but reading your blog is my favorite. You inspire me to never give up. Your blog makes me feel like I don't have to change, I'm okay the way I am. Thank you.

Hugs from Pennsylvania,

Courtney

Chapter Seven
Eleni

Trigger Warning: Suicide, Eating Disorders, Self Harm

Transcription on page 183

This probably the 98752568th letter I am writing to you. I - destroyed every one of the previous letters, beause they did not include enough words to say "Thank You". I think though that words will never be enough. Only I will ever know, how much good you've done to me. And I wanted you to know that I appreciate it. A lot.

People never helped me. It's not that they didn't try. I just ... dislike people. So, no matter how good someone was to me, I would always turn my back. Avoid any human connections I still do. But you... you somehow touched me. Not right away. Besides I first met you on 9gag! When I saw that post, I never imagined that you were a person with a history like that. I would never imagine that we had things in common. At that point, I was a few months away from being 16 and I was cutting myself for the past 4 years. I had broken four bones of my body with a hammer, and I'd already tried to kill myself six times. In one word, I was "hopeless". My ED (bulimia) was at its finest and I was so close in attemting killing myself again. It was meant for that night I had the pills, I had everything I needed. But then I saw your blog, your story. That night I stayed awake. By the morning, the pills were still inside that box and I was still alive. Breathing. Until then, I wasn't actually

1

living. Just surviving through the days, through the events. That day, was the day my life started. I remember being 7 years old. A kid full of joy. Until some other classmates of mine called me fat. Technically my life is paused since then. I wasted 9 years of my youth, hating me. Hating everything about me. It's not fair. That was when I realised it. I started LIVING. I continued my life from the day I paused it. Of course, nothing is the same and it will never be, but I'm so happy to say that I even like myself sometimes. Before depression was home to me and hapiness a place I rarely visited. And I am proud to say that today, things are the other way around. I smile. And after all those years, that smile is real and it doesn't hide any pain. I learned -with you- to express my feelings. I smile because I want to, because I feel like it, because I deserve it. I cry because bad things still happen. You taught me that not all days are gonna be good and that life has its upsides and downs. With your own special, unique, magestic, amazing way you saved me and from the bottom of my heart I thank you. Today I still have my moments. There are times when I still purge what I eat. And I know that these times are going to disappear completely (I wish, I really do). I haven't cut myself or hit myself in the last 4 MONTHS! :D Mostly though, I am thankful that I still have my life. I am here. And after many years I am planning to stay. I wanna come to the U.S and study music performance. I won a piano scholarship for my two last years of High School in a private school. That will make things much easier. And I promise you that I will come at your house the first week I'll arrive at U.S.A.

So, make sure that you will be there. Make sure that you will keep trying, even if some days are darker than the normal. Because you are an inspiration Elijah. To so MANY PEOPLE. Me included. And I wanted you to know that I will be there no matter what. 'Cause I care about you. More than you can understand.

And I love you.

Please never forget that.

I care, I love you, I'm here. And you? You will never ever ever ever gonna have to be alone.

Take Care

Eleni

Chapter Eight
Ellen

Trigger Warning: Suicide, Self Harm, Abuse

Transcription on page 185

Hello, well now that the whole weird greeting is out of the way, I can say thank you. Although I still struggle with self harm and will for awhile, I decided to send some of them to you, razors,[3] that is. In advance I would like to say that I'm sorry for the terrible hand-writting, grammar and some spelling. I would like to say thank you for doing what you've been doing. Also, you and your girlfriend are adorable together, hold on to her while you have her, you never know when today is the last day that you'll see her.

So, I just realized that that made absolutely no sense, sorry about that. I'm just kinda scared, like I have been for the past four years. This stupid journey that I've made myself go through. I don't think that I've ever told someone my story completely before, so bear with me if it seems completely stupid and pointless, but it's what

[3] To see an image of the blades mentioned in this letter, please see pg. 161

has gotten me to this point.

I guess my story begins a year before I was born. My dad was on his way home from a date with my mom when a milk truck ran him over (he was in a small Hundai(?)). They though that he was dead until he moved his arm slightly. In that accident, he was changed forever. He made it out alive but recieved a closed head injury. I don't know if you know anything about head injuries but they're quite awful. Now he has an explosive side which scares the shit out of you.

Don't get me wrong I love my dad, but growing up having to be careful about what you say to your dad is very uneasy feeling. He'd get so stressed out that he'd explode, it was absolutely terrifying. He'd hit me when he got extremely angry. I always deserved it though, I shouldn't have been near him, annoying him.

What scared me is as I was growing (sexually) I remembered things that started to scare me. That was when I realized what had happed. I don't know how long it lasted. I just know it happened enough for me to remember vivid details. Some say that my father is an idiot for doing this and letting it happen, but I personally try to forget it.

In the first grade, I lost my grandfather, my favorite person in the world. It was like I didn't have someone for me anymore. My dad, naturally, fell apart and began to explode more frequently. He would throw things, mostly fans and glass, he would pound on the walls continuosly (?) until a hole had formed. I don't know if he was filled with more pride or shame in everything he had done. But after a few years, it got better... for awhile.

Then in February 2005, my worst nightmare happened. My best friend was diagnosed with Luekemia (not sure if I butchered that word). For five years, I watched her lay in that hospital bed bearly hangin on as the cancer tried to take everything she had. But she won that battle, and things were ok. Until seventh grade when I was diagnosed with clinical depression.

I was always sad, so my mom immedietely sent me to the good old doctor and put me on meds. A few months after my cousin and I were raped by some "friends" of hers. That night still haunts my dreams. I can still hear her screams and feel the hands all over you. That is something, I'd never wish upon anyone, ever.

Then 8th grade came, and everything changed. I broke down completely, lost my happy false exterior and gained a lost, sad, depressed, lonely and scared facad. I tried to be strong, but I couldn't for very long. That was when my relationship with John and my razors began. Both would put me in the hospital and cause me never-ending pain.

I was never very smart when it came to people, school; I could do it, but when someone would have a problem with me, my solution was to ignore them until the probem went "away". I've lost more friends that way than anything else. Is it normal to think about your razor everyday? To reassure yourself that you can cut in just a little while? That things can get better once you cut away your sorrows. All of the memories kept coming back and I couldn't take it anymore.

On February 25, 2011, I was seconds from death. I had had enough of living this hell, so I took a razor and sliced and sliced over and over until my arm didn't have any more room. But, I was still hungry for more, more blood. So I moved to my leg and sliced and sliced. The sight of seeing that open area slowly start to well made me feel... alive. I had sent the goodbye texts and waited for my angel to take me. But all I got was a cop. A friend had called the police.

My dad found out that night that I had been cutting. I've never seen him so distraught, he started crying in the hall while the nurses took my blood pressure. It was horrifying to see my strong 6'6 dad, slide to the ground in tears. Do you know what that does to you? To see the center, rock, of your world fall all because of you?

That day, I saw what was worth living. For a few months I was fine, two months without cutting or attempting suicide. And then it all went to shit. I guess that's how it normally goes, life sees that you're happy and it slaps you around until you give.

I no longer have thoughts (constantly) of suicide, but my cutting has become worse. It's become daily, hourly even. I've gotten to the point where I bring my razors to class, I pull over on the side of the road to relieve the pain, and I can't focus anymore: like right now. I'm in class and all I want to do is cut, hell I just did a minute ago, but it's not enough.

My friends don't understand what this is. They don't get why this is all happening and why I'm putting them through this. To be honest, I don't even know why I'm putting them in this position. I'm terrified, and what is there that I can do? I've been asking myself this question for months until I saw your videos and I knew that maybe, just maybe I could give some of them up. I can't give them all because I think I'd freak out, but I can give you some.

I'm really scared that I can't do this. I know that people have done this and that they've alright now, but I've been struggling for years. How can I give something up that hasn't left me since I got it. Be strong and don't give up like I have. I know that this is beyond stupid of me, but I don't know what do do. My mom's ready to put me in the hospital and I can't even have a door anymore. I'm only 16 and I don't want to be here right now, there has to be some solution. somewhere that can help to change all of this... crap.

It's scary that since I've gotten my license, three months ago, I've bought several, no dozens of razors. Am I the only one who has done this? Am I really that screwed up or is this normal? I don't really know how to stop this. It's like my world's crumbling down around me and I can't rebuild it.

I'm sorry for rambling and I don't expect a reply. But for kicks and giggles my email address is It would be amazing to know that I'm not the only one who has suffered from this

Chapter Nine
Erica

Trigger Warning: Self Harm

Transcription on page 188

You still haven't told me if you read my letters from July / August. I'm in class right now, trying to figure out how to get my school to invite you to speak here. I also don't know whom to talk to about it. I know that we have already established that you will eventually come, because I know you want your bracelet.

It's really bad, because I'm not even sure who my principal is. Even if I did, I wouldn't know how to confront him and say, "There's this guy on the internet that makes videos to make people feel good. He wants to speak at schools and I think we should invite him here". I'm just a little freshman, remember?

I don't know if I can talk to my friends about inviting you because they say I talk about internet people too much... and I guess they're right. They kind of tune out right when I say the word "internet".

Maybe I could try talking to a teacher, but the teacher that I'm closest to is my German teacher. I don't really know what authority she has. She's one of the heads of the Freshman Class, which I guess is something.

Sorry if this doesn't seem well thought out. I only just decided to write this letter. I decided to write it for two reasons. One is by means of procrastination. I *really* do not want to do my work right now. The other is to let you know of basically all I said on the front.

Hope to see you soon,
Erica

P.S. I could feel/see my handwriting getting progressively worse. Sorry.

P.P.S. I knew how to sign it this time! :)

I meant to put that at the end of the other letter. My bad.

(Trigger warning for letter 2. I attempt to talk about my scars.)

I don't really know what to say to you. I feel too awkward to even start this letter in a meaningful way. That's probably not a good sign, considering I'm in journalism class (same class as the last letter) so I should be getting good at writing leads and such.

I want to restart so badly, but then I'll know that I can't even write a little letter to "some guy on the internet" (No offense. That's mostly how my sister refers to you and other tumblr people).

I guess I should start getting to the point now? I don't know how to say this. Sorry if it's just a bunch of random words and sentences. I don't own any blades. I never have. However, I have scars on my hands from about second grade. Most of them are only barely visible, but there was five on my right hand and three on my left that you could see better than the others. Some of the lighter scars are also on my arms. I just counted a total of seven on my arms. The ones on my hands used to be slightly more visible. About two months ago (August 9th) I made the eight scars bleed. Actually, the bleeding wasn't bad, but at least the top layer of skin was gone. They hurt to touch for about a week and a half. Sometimes, when I got mad at myself, I would pick at them to bleed again. I've let them go and am trying my hardest to let them heal. I don't think they're ever going to look like my normal skin again. So far, six of the eight have almost completely healed. There's one on the top of my right wrist and one on my left hand that still need a little bit of time.

As of last night, there's a new, much lighter scar, also on my left hand. It's slightly curved. You may think this is stupid and childish (I know I do) but I bit myself last night. I didn't bite hard enough to break skin. At the time, I wanted to so badly, but I didn't have the guts to do it. Now, I'm glad I stopped. I was just under a lot of stress and I was exhausted (on many levels), but I knew I would just be more mad at myself if I went through with it.

My point is (two paragraphs later) that I can't send you what I've used to hurt myself. Honestly, I never considered it self-harm before recently. Anyway, I can't send you my fingernails or teeth or jaw. I'm the one that has something against myself, not a blade, not a knife, not safety pins, and not a flame. I don't know if you read or will read this whole thing, but thank you. You have no idea how much it means to me to actually have someone that will listen and not judge.

Thank you again,

Erica

P.S. Sorry this is so many words. It took me all of 3rd hour. But it was worth it.

By the time I put this in the envelope, 10-14-12, some of this is irrelevant

Chapter Ten
Grace

Trigger Warning: Suicide, Self Harm

Transcription on page 190

Dear Elijah and Lauren.

My name is Grace, and I'm 13 years old and I live in the UK, England. I'm writing to let you know that by the end of your video, I was crying so much, more than I ever had in my life. I was touched by it, because like some of my friends (Internet Friends!) had viewed it, and we all felt like it was speaking to us. It's one of the loveliest videos I've seen addressing Self Injury. I'm so glad you included an address, because I love to able to contact people who create touching videos!

I've struggled with issues all my life, I've actually injured myself through frustration since I was around 5 years old. It started with hitting and punching, scratching and pulling my own hair. I've always been bullied, and it's impacted so much on me. I've been called nearly every name under the sun, it's safe to say. I never had much luck with friends or love either. I get really paranoid about talking about myself, because I get worried people think I'm self centred so all I'm going to say is that I'm on medication for my Bipolar II, and I suffer with psychotic symptoms when I'm having a manic episode.

People have always seen my problems as attention seeking, and when I got a diagnosis, everyone just takes pity on me. I've tried to commit suicide. It hurt everyone around me and they didn't realise how much mental pain I was in. Anyway. My pulling, punching, hitting and scratching turned to cutting. I made my first cut aged 11. The scars in the video really stuck out to me, because the depression might stop, but the scars will always remain, mental and physical.

I really can't get over how striking your video was. Honest. You and Lauren have basically explained my life. In a video. And I can't thank you enough for how inspiring you are. I don't hurt myself as much now. I have found some ways to deal with my pain, but sometimes it's too overwhelming. So I'm sending you my blades.[4] All of them. Every single one. It's so hard for me to do, but whenever I enter a shop, to steal (yes, that's what my habit has come to) myself some blades, I'm going to think of your video. And walk out the shop, feeling happy with myself. Your video has helped me more than counselling ever has. And I thank you for that. Honestly.

---

[4] To see an image of the blades mentioned in this letter, please see pg. 161

Chapter Eleven
Hannah

Trigger Warning: Suicide, Self Harm

Transcription on page 191

Dear Elijah,

Remember sassy Maddie from [illegible] 'Mail Time 8'? Well she's my best friend and she told me about your video. I just watched 'So You Think You're Worthless?' and... it was exactly what I needed to hear. I'm starting my journey to recovery from depression, cutting, and suicidal thoughts and actions. That's why my razor was included in this. I promised Maddie I wouldn't cut again, I promised my other best friend, and now I'm promising you. Starting today, I'm going to try to be a happy girl! :) And a message that, if you feel like it, I think people should know: Yeah, I know sometimes pain gets so unbearable. Please don't self-Harm. Please don't starve yourself, and PLEASE don't attempt suicide. The consequences definitely aren't worth it.

The end of the message. Thank you Elijah...

Love,

Hannah

P.S. I went from April-August being a cutter. The scars aren't worth it.

Stay Strong

I should be doing AP homework now... :)

Chapter Twelve
Hilary

Trigger Warning: Suicide, Eating Disorders, Self Harm

Transcription on page 192

My name is Hilary and I don't want to be anonymous anymore. I want to feel confident and I want my voice to be heard. I want to be *significant*. I want to *matter*. And I'm on my way there. No matter how long or hard it is, I promise I'll get there.

Thank you, Elijah and Lauren for posting that video on Tumblr. It may just have *turned my life around*. I self harm and I suffer from depression and split personaity. I wish I could send you my blades. I really wish I could! But I actually got rid of them a while back. So I'm sending you this instead. This weird peice of paper is my "inspiration." I made it as an alternative to suicide one night, and each night, I would look at is as an accomplishment. This is the night I decided to recover. I made it in early June, or late May. I did pretty well. I thought I did it.

But when school started, my parents started fighting again. My sister started to abuse me again. And I cracked. I gave in to the urge. I cut my hip on September 19. I don't regret it. Why? Because my cut before that was on June 2. More than 100 days. I'm looking at the bright side. *I didn't cut for 100 days!*

I guess that's just who I am. I like to look at what I've recovered from:

- suicidal tendencies (woohoo! I still have thoughts though)
- anorexia (I actually got up to a healthy BMI Wow!)
- Social anxiety disorder (what is there to be afraid of?)

I'm only 15. I've barely lived! How can I be so sure I want to die when I haven't even *been* anywhere? This stupid fight isn't over until I win, and I have so many years ahead of me to make sure that's exactly what I do!

Anyways, I thought I'd explain my "inspiration"[5] to you so you understand it.

[5] See image at end of chapter.

Basically, this is a statement of "I don't care about my OCD. I'm going to make this how I want it!" Hence the random dot, fabric paper and the badly drawn girl. This is what it means to me:

The stars: The quote "look at the stars, look how they shine for you" was the only quote I could believe. I guess it's because I think the stars are metaphors. Each star represents 1 person who loves you, who will always be there for you, and who is willing to do anything for you. How many stars are out there? Countless...

Faith: To be honest, I'm an Athiest, so I don't know why I put a cross as the t, but it was supposed to mean "have faith in yourself, because you can do it." Faith means that even if you fall, you'll still get back up, knowing this time you'll go longer without falling. And I need that. I really do.

Mistakes / Underestimate: It's okay to make mistakes. We all make them. It isn't the end of the world or your life. Just a bump in the road. And do not ever underestimate people. Chances are, most of them are suffering a similar battle, and who are you to question their strength?

"Here's an umbrella" "Thanks": This is sort of in the format of a text message. Kind of like person 1 is saying to person 2, "hey, I know what you're going through. Maybe I can help?" Like person 1 is giving person 2 an umbrella for the rain. Again, metaphor.

Gold pen quote: "anything worth undoing ain't worth doing." was the quote of my life when a boy named Jeremy bullied me nearly to death in grade 8. He tried to apologize to me after I missed a few days of school because of him. "I didn't know." "It was a joke." Were his excuses. But it's no use. Those things he said to me... They're a part of me forever now. I lost 10 months of memories because of him. I can't remember 2011 at all because I was in so

much shock. I will never forget those nights he tore my life apart.
Hope over fear: Recovery is scary. It's absolutely terrifying. But I'm getting used to it. Because the only thing stronger than fear is hope. With hope, I know, that against all odds, I *can* do it. I *can* recover.

Taped up blade[6]: This one is my favourite of them all. I used this blade to cut myself. I also used this blade to cut a piece of paper until it was so dull, it couldn't cut my skin, no matter how hard I tried. I won. I won the battle for now. So I took my useless, dull, defeated blade and I taped it to my "inspiration" like a trophy. *I won that round.* I killed the blade. The blade died. Its funeral. Not mine.

But the battle isn't over. I'm not anywhere near recovered. *Far* from it. I don't know if I'll ever get better. The scars are too deep, and the voices *always* come back. But like I said: I'm 15, and I'm not giving up. I know it's bad that I broke my self-harm free streak, but today is day 3, and I'm trying again. This time, 150 days. I can do it. I know I can. I'm on this Earth for a reason, and I'm going to find it. I'm going to keep going. I'm going to survive. Because I am strong. Strength to me is the ability to stay alive, survive 12 years of constant bullying, qualify for the Olympics and look Jeremy in the eye and smile. He couldn't kill me. *Nothing* can. I'm too broken. I'm simply unfixable. Fine. It's a challenge.

And, of course, I have to thank *you* for giving me hope. I remember watching your video on how "skinny doesn't get you anything" and there I was, frail, off-season Hilary, weighing at 90 lbs, starving. You killed my voices. Whatever they said, you were *stronger*. And I was able to gain the weight back and be healthy. Now I'm hovering around 110 lbs! Healthy enough. Anyways, as I was watching your video, I was crying. I couldn't stop. Because of you, I was able to recover from anorexia. Hopefully, you can help me recover from 11 years of self-harm. (Yes, I've been self-harming since I was 4. It only got bad when I was 12) But I'm going to do it, whatever it takes. Thank you, Elijah, I can never thank you enough for saving my life.

[6] To see an image of the blade mentioned in this letter, please see pg. 161

I may just be an insignificant face in Toronto, but I have a dream and a hell of a lot of determination. I don't care how many times I fall. I *will* get back up. And I will not stop until an Olympic gold medal is hanging around my neck. I will thank Jeremy for telling me I can't. Because without him, I never really would have had the fight to begin with.

"Don't cry because of what you've been through. *Smile*, because of what you *got* through." - Me

"Fall down 7 times, stand up 8." - Unknown

"They tore me apart, I'm back at the start, but I guess that's better than the end." - Me

"You were given this life because you are strong enough to live it." - Unknown

No matter how bad it gets, I'll always have those 100 days. My life is far from finished. It's barely getting started. I have an entire life of opportunity and an unfinished bucket list to complete. I can't wait to get out there and *Live*.

Thank you so much for reading all of that. I know it was long. Stay Strong. I believe in you. My "inspiration" keeps me strong. I just hope it will do the same for you.

Take care,

Hilary

Hilary's "Inspiration" mentioned on page 78

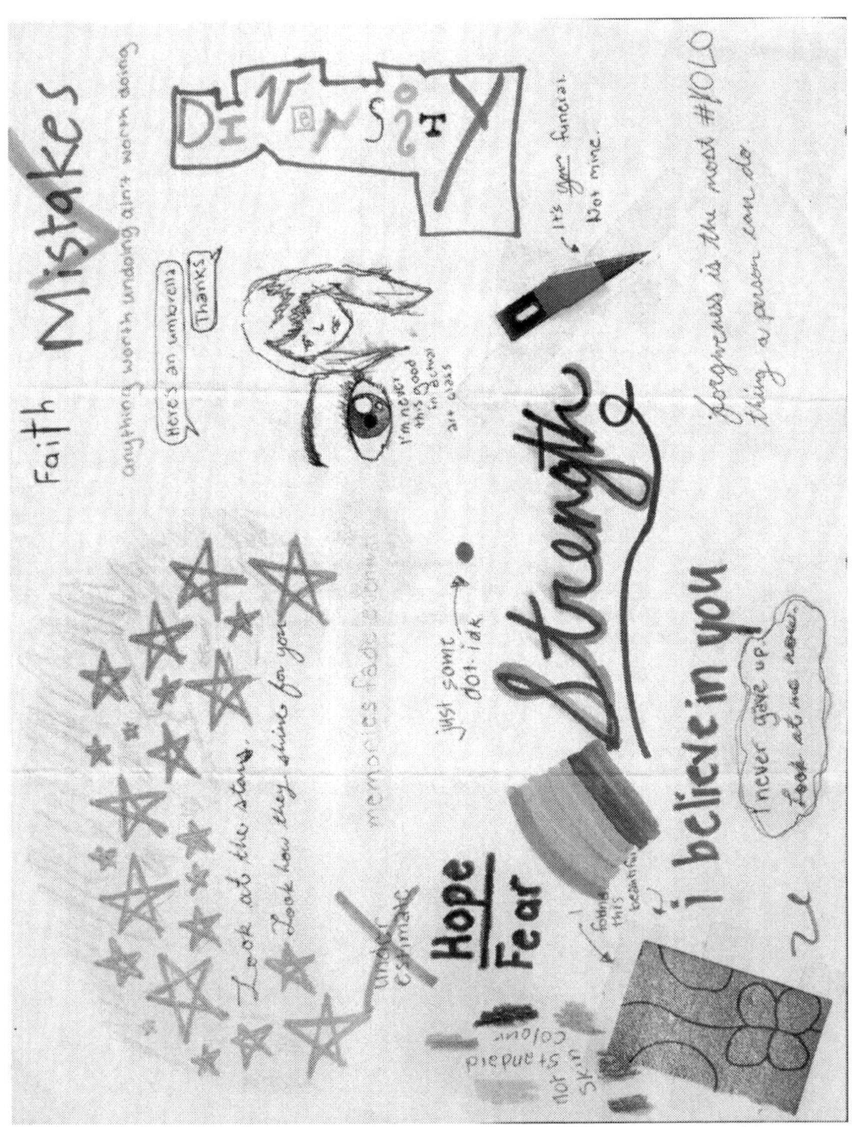

Chapter Thirteen
Jani

Trigger Warning: Suicide, Eating Disorders, Self Harm

Transcription on page 195

why hello there. Elijah? I guess?
so I watched the self harm video where you said to send you blades, but I realized that wouldn't do too much because while I have blades I like, when it comes down to it, anything and everything could be a weapon. this actually came right after I relapsed and have been thinking about this stuff a lot. but realistically, the blades leave the scars, but it's the stuff in your head that really hurts you. So I decided to participate by sending a letter instead. You can't tell by this shitty example, but I'm actually a terrific pen pal. I've just never written to someone I dont actually know before. oh and I suck at socializing. so uh yeah... I think that's all of the disclaimers I have for you.
Hi. I am your dime a dozen basket case of a #foreveralone recovering anorexic. I've got a list of diagnoses a mile long (well, depending on the font size) but I don't like them because to me they're just labels that help the other PHDs understand how my head works better. so Im not including those. good. that's out of the way. um. yes. Im a cutter. no. I don't have a clue why writing you sounded like a good idea, because I don't know what to say and tbh, I wouldn't write me back anyway. I'm a ballerina, I'm a rock climber, I have a min pin named Sharky who's adorable as all get out and who's my Emotional Support Animal, uhh I don't know what else is note worthy... I go to the U of Utah majoring in Ballet and PRT (Parks Recreation, Tourism) ~~and~~ with an emphasis in Adventure & Outdoor Programs (basically a degree in playing outside) and hopefully i'll start my 3rd major next semester which is EMS.

God only knows why I'm telling you all of this. I followed you a while back after yet another relapse when I stumbled upon one of your videos. But, I'm a really shitty follower cuz I don't stalk your blog like I probably should so I really don't know much about you except that your girlfriend is adorable. and pretty. (you should pass that on)

idk. I was a good follower for like a day and sent you a message so I'm a winner. I've now irritated you on 2 kinds of media. yay.

So uh the purpose of this letter? I guess I could turn it into fan mail because I feel people should be praised when they do good, and you do. but really, I needed something to do to pass some time while I have so much suicidal ideation and without a distraction I might think it into action.

So there you have it, I am using you. Hopefully you don't mind, which you shouldn't because if you don't want to read it you could always just trash it.

So uh tumblr.... let's talk fandoms. Guess you could say I'm Supernatural, BTVS, Firefly, idk i'm sure there's lots more than that, making a list was harder than I thought haha

in any case... um here is a shark because this is from your self harm video and apparently self injury shark is a thing.

oh fun fact: I can't draw for beans but I usually do anyway.

Are you anywhere near Duluth? one of my best friends is from there... anywho I guess I'll let you get back to your life and the real world now. Send me a letter some time if you ever feel like pen paling it up or need to rant or whatever.

♡Jani

Chapter Fourteen
Jen

Trigger Warning: Self Harm
Transcription on page 197

You my dear are an inspiration to so many people, and that includes myself. I want to tell you, Im not afraid to tell my story anymore. And Im starting with telling <u>you</u> my story, because I remember that you care. I know we've never met and probably never will, but thats okay, as long as I know theres someone out there who cares. So heres my story if youre willinginginy to listen. Ive struggled through depression and anxiety and self harm since grade five. Of course in grade five when I bruised myself on purpose. I didnt know it was self harm. All I knew was that I was upset and I needed to get away from it. In grade five I didnt even think Id turn out like I did.

In grade six I started cutting myself. I dont remember exactly what gave me the idea to cut, but I did, and I still regret the day I decided to pick up that blade. Some guys found out what I did and they started messaging me, saying I was a freak, they called me emo. Some of them told me they'd come to school and shove a Snickers bar down my throat. (Im deathly allergic to all nuts) They said they'd take care of killing me, so I didnt have too. I took the bus home in middle school, those same boys were on my bus and got off at the same stop as me. They'd walk behind me and throw rocks at my head. Last year in grade nine, things almost seemed to get better, then I relapsed. I had to go to mental health, and see a specialist... In may of last year I was admitted to the hospital. In the hospital I had two guards with me at all times. They watched my every move. They heard me cry at night. The bathrooms didnt lock and there was no shower curtain, it was like they could have come in at any moment. I wasnt allowed my worry stone, I wasnt allowed bracelets... I wasnt even allowed to wear my own underwear.

Some guys at my school started treating me like an object. I'd just broken up with my boyfriend and these guys had been annoying me, they were kind of my friends... so as a joke I said if you stop annoying me I'll give you a free boob squeeze. I thought they knew I was joking. They took it ~~lit~~ literally. They even told some other friends about it. I'd have random guys come up to me in the hall and touch my boobs. I know in a way its my fault, but I still feel violated by them.

I try and smile more these days. My boyfriend and I recently celebrated our one year. I know I should be happy, I know other people have it worse than me. But Im still constantly tormented by the dark parts of my mind. My self harms gotten so much worse now... and I dont know what to do. My arms are covered in scars... they're getting harder to hide...

Please dont think badly of me for what Ive told you... I know Ive made mistakes in life, and Im trying to do better, but its hard when I feel like dying everyday. Its hard to get better and recover when it's so easy to just pick up the blade.

I just want you to know, Im trying very hard to stay alive. Im still in this fight; and I dont want to give up...

Thanks for caring
Love Always,
-J

Chapter Fifteen
Julia

Trigger Warning: Suicide, Eating Disorders, Self Harm

Transcription on page 199

Hi,

Umm... I'm Julia, and I'm 16. I've actually started this letter a few times. I didn't know what to write about or how to explain myself. Welp, I hate myself every thing about myself. I'm too fat, I'm not smart enough. I'm not good at anything but screwing up. You don't seem to mind people's stories and I've never told my whole story before so... here goes nothing. July 13th 1996 a girl was born after 2 days of labor and ending with a C-section. At this time her parents an her lived in New York. Her father was able to support the three of them fairly well. Until her brother was born. Mom and Dad both had to work, and this meant moving to Florida. Julia was five years old. Gradek was fine as every five year old deserves to be happy. 1st was okay. 2nd her little sister was born not long before Christmas. Then was the accident. The accident that started a chain reaction that changed everything. My dad drove tractor trailors, he was a truck driver. One day the person who loaded his truck did it wrong. He was going to unload it, and every thing inside of it fell on him. Today it was bank safes that he was transporting. There were three that really screwed him up. He was always in pain, and with what happened he should have been paralyzed. After this he tried to work for most of third grade. There was the one really big fight that I walked onto when my dad threw the peanut butter and jelly jars across the kitchen. Other than that our year was fairly good. Fourth grade started off okay. In my school the Tuesday before Thanksgiving we had Grandparents day. And being in fourth grade on Grandparents Day meant you got to be in the play! My dad promised he would video tape it. He didn't. He had ODed the night before. It's so scary being nine years old and seeing your father, who only seems to be asleep, being carried away on a strecher one day before Thanksgiving. He was in the hospital for two months. Nobody told me anything so, of course I asume I did everything wrong and got all As for the rest of the year. I just wanted them to stop fighting. They didn't. Dad moved out mom filed for diverce. In fifth grade a boy told me I was fat and ugly. Great self confidence booster. The Summer after I decided I wanted to be tiny so I ate every other day, and binged every other day. Sixth grade was the most stable year except for the fact I had no friends. That Summer was the first time I wanted to really die, and

I would have. 4 bottles of Advil. 20 [illegible] tylenol. My mom's current boyfriend had made me feel like I should die. I wanted nothing more than to Show him how low he made me feel. To bad my mom noticed how hurt I was, and made me spend the night with her. The next night was the first time I cut. Then was seventh grade when my life was looking up mom was going to A.A. she was single but a bitch without her morning vodka and evening rum. In October my dad was getting sick again. Nobody would notice that didn't live with him. Thank God I only lived with him every other weekend and Wendesdays. He started smoking more and more pot and taking more and more pain killers. He was falling more, and sometimes I would have to go outside put out his half-smoke joint, and attempt to drag him inside. My sister [illegible] [illegible] had just turned 5 and my brother was 7 I was 12 and it was December 3^1st at 8:20 A.M my father was pronounced dead. He had over dosed on the 28th My siblings didn't know until the 2nd. I remember everyone wanted me to make all these decisions, but nobody would let me do anything. My mom wasn't allowed to do anything as their divorce had been completed not to long before. For about 4 months I

I lied about how hurt and sad I was. I threw myself into school work tried out for cheerleading and decided I was going to be skinny. 8th grade was the year I was a cheerleader it was a girl on the cheer team with me who taught me about total self destruction. She introduced me to "naughty" social networking sites. She taught me then set me loose. I was 13. I was cutting every night, taking naked pictures every night, staying up till 3AM having phone sex. My mom thought I was on drugs. Then cheerleading ended. My dad was still dead I was still ugly. But hey I had random guys all random ages telling me how beautiful I was if I took pictures for them. Febuary my mom noticed my arms, and noticed how sad I was. She took away my phone and promised if she ever saw another cut she would make me live with my grandparents. I stopped for a while. Freshman year Thanksgiving morning, my mom and I got in the worst fight ever. We were on our way to morning Mass and she made me get out and walk home. I got home went to the medicine ~~cabinet~~ cabinet and took everything I could find. Around 4 o'clock that day I couldn't breath, they made me go to the hospital, they asked me what I did. I was sent into a 72 hour lockdown at the mental hospital. I didn't eat nor sleep, and I told them what they wanted to hear. The doctor told me to think more clearly. I shook it all off went back to school. My mom punished me for wanting to die. She took away computer and phone again. In March she told me I could switch schools. My best friend and I switched together. I was clean from everything till December. December I met this boy who introduced me to Mary Jane. I stopped going to school. Then for Christmas I got a laptop, and before to long I was back to 8th grade but worse. That boy would make me feel like an ugly nothing. So I went online and online boys were so much nicer if you were nice to them. I was on webcam doing things that made me feel like nothing, but at least I was pretty. Thats what they said. What they promised. But my grades fell fast and I was always high then my grandma died and I had to be strong for everyone to replace what my dad couldn't do because he's dead. I was crying myself to sleep I was cutting. I wanted to die. Over the summer I "got my act together" then there was the bus accident. July 13th my 16th birthday I was in a church bus driving to Atlanta, Georgia. 10 seconds we side-swiped a horse trailer with all of our stuff in it. I got the worst of it. Niched my left arm artery, glass in my muscles, and I was scared that the 8 year old I had in my lap was hurt. Out of everything I had never been so scared. My mom home in Florida. Nobody knew if I was going to be okay or not. My "friends" when I got home were laughing like it was a joke. I started cutting again. I have been cutting. I do cry myself to sleep every night. There has been nothing "naughty" from me since the accident. I just wish it had killed me. Now here I am sitting in math class and it took me 4 days to write this letter.

I'm[7] giving you my story and my razors. Thank you so much.

Julia

[7] To see an image of the razors mentioned in this letter, please see pg. 161

Chapter Sixteen
"K."

Trigger Warning: Self Harm

Transcription on page 203

Hi,

I don't really know if you will read this or not, but if you happen to, I just want to say thank you... thank you for posting a video that I had come across on tumblr and made me feel so inspired to let go of this object[8] that had helped bring the pain to my skin. I know by sending away this object that holds so many dark memories I can now begin to let go and move on. I won't be able to harm myself anymore. I hope you know, you are helping a person, and many others too that need somewhere to begin cleaning up their lives. It may be the first or the last time, but this has helped majorly and I'm looking forward to a healthy future.

Thanks again, K

[8] To see an image of the blade mentioned in this letter, please see pg. 161

Chapter Seventeen
Kaitlyn

Trigger Warning: Suicide, Eating Disorders, Self Harm

Transcription on page 204

my name is Kaitlyn I'm 14 years old, and I want to share my story with you.
on July 27, 2007, I purged for the first time. I was 10 years old. I knew it was bad, so I promised myself I would never do it again. Three weeks later, I broke that promise. shortly after that, I began cutting myself. I used whatever I could get my hands on, sometimes having to rely on my finger nails. my weight dropped drastically and for a 10 year old, I was extremely underweight. I tried to pull myself out of the pit that I was being pushed into, and made it out for a while. I didn't self harm for a few months, I didn't purge for 3 months! in february of 2008, I started again, falling back into habits I thought I had broken. no one found out, i kept going. for two more years, I continued hurting myself →

then, on December 18, 2010, I told my friend stephanie, (a college age girl who went to my church) that I cut. She told me that if I didn't tell my mom, she would. I told my mom that night, she was furious, and put me in counseling with our pastor. This pastor did nothing to help me because he didn't understand.

I stopped, until January 2011; where I picked up my bad habits again. By this time, my cuts were getting deeper, leaving scars. My parents made me join a swim team, which only resulted in teasing from the coaches and other swimmers, so I cut where they wouldn't see it; in my stomach. I kept going, until February 2nd, 2011. I was so fed up with everything I just wanted to die. at 3 am, crying, shaking, terrified, I wrote my suicide notes. one to my little brother, one to my parents, one to

my best friend. I took 30 pain killers, laid down on the floor. I was 13 years old.
15 minutes later, I felt sick. I crawled to the bathroom, forced myself to throw up until I was dry heaving, and realizing that I didn't really want to die. I went on living my miserable life for another year, until January 2012. My very best friend told me she had beed molested by her brother over 40 times, and that she also cut. I was devastated, and shortly after telling me, she told her parents, and on February 8, she was informed she would be spending the next 8 months in an inpatient treatment facility, and that we would have no contact. I cried, and was heartbroken at the thought of losing her for 8 months. The next day, I was feeling awful about everything tha was going on. I began searching my room for the

blades I knew were hiddn there in the process of searching, I found a book titled "100 favorite Bible verses" I tossed it aside, but then picked it up and flipped through it for the first time. Philippians 4:13 "I can do all things through Christ who gives me strength." I began to cry, and realized, for the first time in my life that there is a God who cares about me, who loves me, who died for me. I found all 86 blades hidden around my room, walked to the family room where my mom was reading and fell into her arms, giving her the blades telling her everything the last 4 years had held, I told her I wanted help. I was put in counseling, soon after, I went to the doctor for a physical. I weighed in at 96 lbs a very unhealthy weight for someone my height. That day, I was diagnosed with Bulimia, severe depression, and severe anxiety. There was talk of sending me to inpatient treatment, nutritionists, specialists. I was anemic underweight, sad, unhealthy, and I regretted asking for help. I saw 2 nutritionist, an ED specialist, my regular doctor, and a therapy once a week for the first 3 months of treatment, and I still do.

I'm proud to say that I'm recovering, with your help, God's help, and the support of my friends and family.

On my birthday, July 24, it will be one month since I self-harmed, and 3 weeks since I purged. (Big improvement, considering a year ago, I was cutting 3-10 times a day and purging everything I ate.)

The time to recover is **NOW.**

I've shared this testimony with two youth groups in the area as well as my tumblr and facebook. My goal is to help someone who is struggling like I am.

I guess the point of this letter is to tell you that there is hope. You may not see it now, you may not feel like it, but there is hope, and you will get through this battle.

Recovery isn't easy,
but it's worth it.

Kaitlyn

i can do all things through Christ who gives me strength. Philippians 4:13 ♡

Chapter Eighteen
Kaity

Trigger Warning: Suicide, Eating Disorders, Self Harm, Abuse

Transcription on page 206

Elijah ,

I don't even know how to start this letter . You're such an inspiration . Your story is truly amazing § you're wonderful . You should never feel sad . I know that isn't possible § it's not fair , but I'm not asking you to make it possible . I know you can't help it , but I can't stand to see someone as inspirational as you upset . It makes me sad .

You've helped me get through so much , whether you know it or not . Some of the times when you were on tinychat , I joined to have something to distract me from cutting . It always worked . When I'm sad I usually scroll through your blog for a while . You help so many people on a daily basis § I just want to say thank you . From them § from me , thank you .

I really wanted to send you my blades , too ... but I couldn't . It was too hard . I promise you that I will though , so they will never hurt another person again . Eventually .

You deserve the best , so don't settle for anything other than that . By the way , good luck with Lauren . :D § if you don't get this package until after the fair thingy § the puzzle pieces § all that adorable stuff , I hope everything went well . :D

Sorry , I couldn't resist mentioning it . It's so adorable . Omg . I can't . sdklfjlak;j .

Okay , I'm transitioning back into my tumblr talk , it's 4:38am , § I'm tired . I really wanted this to be longer , but I have to go to the post office tomorrow § I need sleeeeeeep . Ugh . Sorryyyy . I'll write you again sometime . :3

Remember , it's okay to stumble sometimes . It's okay to relapse . It's okay to say that you're not okay . You can be broken , as long as you promise to try § put the pieces back together .♥

Bye !

Alright, story time. :3

Erm, I've never really told my story before, so I don't exactly know how to start. I guess I'll start at what really caused my start on self-harm.

When I was six, my uncle molested me. He was the first person to ever say anything truly horrible to me, but he made it sound like a compliment. He told me I was lucky. Lucky that he was doing that to me, because there was no way anyone else ever would. He called me names & hit me. He was the first person to ever call my worthless. When I started crying he yelled more & saud that sowing emotion was weak & that I shouldn't cry because it made me even uglier. I believed every word he said.

When I got home I was too embarrassed to say anything, so my family doesn't know. I don't think they ever will since we don't talk to my uncle anymore (for other reasons). You're actually one of the few people who know now.

Anyway, after that it just kinda went downhill. I started punching, biting, pinching, & anything else I could do to hurt myself because I thought I deserved it. I actually tried to break my arm once. If I hurt someone else, I hurt myself. If I did something wrong, I hurt myself.

Mistakes weren't allowed.

I felt dirty. Not physically, but in a way that I can't even describe. In a way where a million showers couldn't help. I felt like I wasn't good enough § like I didn't belong in my school, in my house, like I shouldn't even be alive. At the time I was eight years old. No one should *ever* be thinking about suicide, especially not when they're eight years old. It's quite sad, really. Since I was so young, the only thing I could do to try to end my life was attempt to drown myself in the bathtub, which obviously never worked out.

I'd like to say that I got better from there on, that the self-harm stopped, but it didn't. It got worse, actually. When I was twelve, I realized that I wanted, needed, more pain. The only way I could think of was cutting myself. I hadn't heard anything about it at that point, so I didn't know other people did it. I didn't know that it could § would become addicting. I was twelve, I didn't know anything about anything, but I did know that I wanted to hurt myself.

So I took a kitchen knife § I cut into my skin. I didn't know what to feel. It hurt a lot, but at the same time, it cleared my head. I hadn't been able to think clearly in a long time. Cutting felt like a breath of fresh air.

The cuts started as small scratches, barely even visible. Over time the got worse, a lot worse. The small scratches turned into cuts which turned into gashes which turned into gaping wounds that I had to keep bandaged for weeks before they healed .

Almost cutting to deep and barely staying alive became a habit. At the time, I didn't even care. People knew something was wrong. I wasn't eating, couldn't sleep, barely said a word. Anyone with common sense would know something was wrong, but they didn't do anything about it.

My first real suicide attempt was earlier this year , towards the beginning of January . I don't really remember much of what happened , but I know that I simply walked upstairs , said goodnight to my parents § told them I loved them , then I grabbed three bottles of pills from the bathroom .

I lined the pills up in a row on my desk , I was going to crush them up in a glass of water but I wanted a chance to back out if I changed my mind . I turned on some music § I swallowed the first pill . In five minutes , I had swallowed half the row . There were tears streaming down my face § I was doing everything I could to concentrate on what I was supposed to be doing , ending my life . I had finished all the pills in ten minutes , and by that time I was getting dizzy § there were black spots in front of my eyes . I laid on my bed , closed my eyes , § everything went dark .

Then I woke up .

The next few days were a blur . All I know is that I was violently ill every time I tried to move . My parents wanted to take me to the Emergency Room but I convinced them that it was just food poisoning or the flu . I didn't know what went wrong , why I had woken up . I was supposed to be dead . I was supposed to be free . I was supposed to be free of the pain . I had killed my soul , but my body remained here to suffer .

I attempted two more times within the next six months , both obviously failing . It didn't even matter because I was already dead . I didn't need a gun , or a noose , or pills to tell me that . I had no personality , no friends , no motivation , I was nothing .

On August 2nd , 2012 , I don't know what changed , I don't know what happened but I decided that I wasn't going to be a waste of space anymore . I started playing piano & violin again . I started to draw again , too . I was slowly becoming who I used to be .

I started the Butterfly Project , the Paper Chain Project , & even made recovery bracelets in hopes of recovering . I've relapsed a couple times , but I'm determined to get better . I want to fix myself .

I might have scars on my arms , shoulders , stomach , thighs , & hips , but at least they're scars . & that's all they'll ever be now . They're a part of me that I'm proud to have because they symbolize a battle with myself that I've finally won . I do have moments of doubt , but everyone does. It's part of the process. I'm finally happy again, § I can say that without hesitation.

There are a lot of people who have helped me along the way. Sadly, most of them don't live anywhere near me, but they've still managed to help more than anyone I know in real life. Most of them I actually met on Tumblr § we're really close now. They don't live in the same place as me, but I'm glad that I actually have people I can trust again. It's definitely helped a lot to know I have people to turn to when I want to relapse.

Even though I've struggled with cutting, depression, suicide, § an EDNOS (that's another long story, so I won't go into that), it's good to know that it does get better § everyone should be around to see that.

Chapter Nineteen
Katie

Trigger Warning: Suicide, Eating Disorders, Self Harm

Transcription on page 210

I HAVE CHEMICAL DEPRESSION

Dear Elijah,

I would like to tell you my story. Hi, my name is Katie I'm 19 and I'm a dreamer. I have attempted suicide ~~12 times~~, but as of 10-15-12 I took a new realization of my life: I can't achieve my dreams if I'm dead.

My Story: I ~~HAVE~~ AM BIPOLAR

It started when I was 12, 7th grade. I got called ~~fat~~, ~~ugly~~, a poser. etc. it got to the point that I would cry myself to sleep everynight. So I started to cut. Then after a month I stopped because I was a lead in the school musical, but I was still hurting so I took on the rubberband & just punching ~~myself~~. I did that up until my freshman year. ~~Attempted suicide: 6~~

That's when I started drinking ~~and~~ my pain away. It didn't last long because people still called me ugly, ~~fat~~, ~~worthless~~. So I started starving myself. When people started questioning why I wasn't eating, I started eating but ended up ~~throwing~~

it all up. I was bullemic until the end of sophomore year. I finally had good friends that loved me.

I got my heart broken my sophomore & junior year so I started using the rubberband again, but I stopped when my BFF asked me too. Attempted Suicide: 2

Now comes the sad part: My freshman year of college I was sexually harrased, almost raped, I was in so much pain so I started to cut again. I sat in my jakuzzi and cut so I could die. Someone ended showing up so I ended up leaving. Then the guy that harrased me stalked me for 2 weeks so I decided to take pills, but I ended up eating bad sushi so I threw it all up. I ended up quiting school and went back home. I live with my sister and I got an email from someone to just go kill myself

So I took pills again, but I woke up. Then on July, 23rd, 2012 I cut again to die. I'm obviously still alive. I am getting better slowly but surely. Attempted suicide: 4

Your videos are so hauntingly BEAUTIFUL.

I am staying alive because of One Direction, on one of my suicide attempts What makes you beautiful played. So I am alive because of them. My dream is to meet them. My biggest dream though is to be a singer. I have videos on youtube & I am trying out for the X-Factor.

I just want to say thank you for caring. It's because of you I am fighting for my dreams & my life. Thank You!

♡ Katie

Chapter Twenty
Meg

Trigger Warning: Suicide, Eating Disorders, Self Harm

Transcription on page 211

i'm writting you this letter because i didnt no how else to thank you I know its not much, but i cant afford to send you a big package from England.
Ok so this might sound cliche but you really are amazing, you have been threw stuff that no one should have to go threw and you have come out a better person, you really are so strong.

I'm sorry that i can not even make you a bracelet. I think you have enough, and im shit at that sort of thing anyway, i'm not really any good at anything.

Well im sure i have probably been really annoying you on Twitter, but i have told you things that i havn't ever told anyone else, and if you think im being stupid or whatever, but i just, i cant change the way i feel about myself, you can tell me i'm beautiful, or that i deserve happieness, but it doesnt change the fact that everyday i will be told im ugly and fat, that im worthless and all the rest of it.

I am meant to be doing my college work as i have 5 essays to do, but i decided you are more important. I have never met anyone who cares about other people as much as you do!

Im sorry that im not strong enough to send you my blades because without them i wouldnt be able to stay here, and i cant send you my suicide letter because i might need it, because i'm really not strong. However, if i do get threw this, when i have a baby i will name him or her Elijah, because your the one who tried to help me, your the one who told me i was good enough, and i know i dont believe you, but i am thankfull, i really am. I know that this is just a stupid letter from a girl who has shit hand writting and cant spell but, i wanted to say thankyou, and not just on twitter or tumblr. Elijah i am so so proud of you, you have come so far, and you are so strong to be honest without you i would be dead right now. I know you said you didnt want me to be the person you couldnt save, and i no i just a second ago said i wouldnt, but i will send you my suicide letter, because i want to get better for you, i cant send you my blades because they are what help me stay alive, I will stop smoking for you though, if you want me to I will send you my story, it is not very special, or anything but if you want it I can send it to you.

in all your video's you say "i'm sorry" and it breaks my heart to see you get upset because you cant help, everyone, people send you there blades, I need you to make sure you do not get triggered and that they really dont ever hurt anyone agian.

You told me that other people "broke my brain" but I dont think they did, I cant blame other people for my issues, it is my own fault I cut, its my fault im ugly and fat, im discusting and thats just the truth.

Because im shit at everything I have this picture with your quote on I Dunno why.

even though im sending you my suicide letter I can not promise you I wont write another one but im going to try.

If your reading this its probably to late, I probably really did it, im Sorry everyone, I really am, I just couldnt do it anymore, please nobody blame yourself, its not your fault, im so so sorry I just couldn't do it anymore, I dont talk to anyone or tell you how I feel im Sorry. Im not gunna write an 8 page long thing explaining, because it doesnt matter, its not important, im gone now and I wont be coming back, I will be looking down on you all, forever, I am so Sorry I did this, I dont no what else to say, you can carry on with your life like it was before just without me, im so sorry everyone. I just cant do this any more im not strong enough, it all hurts to much and its not getting better, nobody cry, please, im not worth your tears.

im so sorry I love you all.
love from megan.
xxxx.

ps: goodbye, sorry.

pps: you cant hurt me anymore, because I did this to myself.

oh please wear pink to my funarel? it would mean alot! xxx.

Chapter Twenty One
Parris

Trigger Warning: Suicide, Self Harm

Transcription on page 213

Hi Elijah, I hope your having a great day. :) I apologize in advance if I spell things wrong, I'm not the greatest speller. My name is Parris, and I'm a huge fan of yours, I've watched all your videos + I check your tumblr about everyday. I sent you a few messages on tumblr, but you never replied. I'm sorry for sending them, cuz I didn't realize how many you get, the other day you said you had about 5,000. I figured sending an actual piece of mail would be less bothersome, for you get less mail that way. You inspire me you really do, not because your overcoming your struggles, but because of how you are. You made a blog it got popular + people began to ask you for help, and you don't get mad and be like read my FAQ, are you fuckin stupid, no you actually try to help them, even though its not your job. And I know I don't know you, I've only come to a conclusion of how you are from your blog + your videos, so if I'm totally wrong or come off as rude, I'm sorry. This is going to address some of the points in your post with a picture of you (which I think looks good, cuz I think you have really pretty eyes), and it starts with 'This is going to be a selfish post where I talk about myself' (which its not 'selfish' cuz its your blog, and you can post whatever the fuck you want) Thats another thing, I tend to write how I speak, and when I speak I tend to swear alot, so I'm sorry if it comes off wrong or you take offense. Anyways you don't look awful, agian you have really pretty eyes, and iono if your sick or just feel bad or sad, it doesn't matter I hope you feel better. I'm sure you'll finish with Laurens gift, and even if you don't she seems like the type of person who would truley appreate the effort you put into it. (I stalk her blog aswell, and I think you've got a good one there, don't let that go) I don't know why you havn't been to work, but thats ok, just relax and don't stress it, it'll all be fine. I really hope that you were able to fight the self-harm urges, and if you did end up self-harming, its ok, you're still a beautiful human being, and you can come back from it. I couldn't imagine trying to fight it with people sending blades, thats another reason I find you so inspirational, is even with that you still want people to send them to you, you want to help them. I don't know how you handle the urges or control it, but the strange thing I do is I take a tak and I kinda chew on the plastic side where the metal pokey part isn't in your mouth or isn't poking you or anything, and iono, I know its pretty weird, but it kinda makes me feel comfortable or safe, I'm not really sure how to explain it, but because its there I don't really get those urges as much. Iono I was just thinkin that might help you a bit. Even if you don't want to eat, you should anyway, cuz I figure your just like ehhh food, but just eat some stuff anyway. Nobody knows what to do all the time, and not knowing is ok, you'll figure it out eventually. I think your really stressing or sort of panicing about the fact you don't know what to do, for you put it 3 times. And again I can't stress enough how **OK** it is to not know, knowing isn't important, just do what you feel is right. I don't know all thats happening in your life right now, but I think maybe your need to help people is a factor to why your depresson may be coming back. I think in your head you've set a bar for yourself, thats really high maybe because people keep telling you that you are so great and inspiradtional, and help them so much, they trust you, and go to you for help. So you feel like your task is the help people, but so many people come to you, its not possible to help so many people. And knowing that these people, come to you, some with thier lives, you try your best to help + do what you can, but your only one peson. You can't help everyone, and I think thats whats starting to get to you. Just know that helping just one peson is something to be proud of. You impact peoples lives in a positive way and thats something to be proud of. Theres not this huge expectation of you, people you actually know, and your followers are aware you have your own shit to deal with, you don't live for us, you need to take care of yourself + the ones closest to you first. Would you like to be able to take care of everyone, sure, but you can't. Its not that we (people of the internet, your followers + whatnot) are putting the expectation on you that your an inspirational blog/help blog, its not that we see your blog that way, its how we see you. You inspire people, because of your genuine wanting to help people, for some reason it seems so pure hearted, and your ability to do that/feel that way, and still struggle, that is what is inspiring to people. Because you've struggled/ing + are overcoming it, makes people feel as if you get it, you understand what they are feeling + can help them, in addition they feel that pure hearted want/need to help, that is why people come to you for help. You follow the advice of your heros/icons right?, well some people see you as such, + want the advice of their hero : Elijah. Another reason people come to you is you seem like you don't judge, and no one wants to feel like they are being judged, its one of the worst feelings in the world. I know that your prolly kinda scared to have shit

coming back, and maybe feeling a bit helpless cuz you don't think be there for people and your letting everyone down. Its fuckin OK, your not letting anyone down, i think everyone knows your doing the best you can. And the little things you do for people, they matter alot, what you do, more like how you are is appreciated. No one ever seems ok, because no one is, everyone struggles with something no matter how big or how small. If your really set on speaking at a school, you might be able to speak at mine, though I live far from you. I go to Midwest City Highschool, Oklahoma, the number is 405-739-1741, and the address is 213 Elm Street, Midwest City, Ok 73110. Idono how to go about any of that, but if you want there the information. If you happen to need to talk, there's so many people that care about you, who would love to talk to you and care about you, such as your girlfriend, but if you end up needing someone I'm here. You are an amazing and beautiful human being, have a great day, and a long wonderful life. (ツ) Oh + I'm really sorry its so long or if you hate it or if this was bothersome or annoying, or you somehow get offended, I'm sorry + yeah.
To end on a lighter and humorous note:
Mother mother fuck. Mother mother fuck fuck. Mother fuck mother fuck.
Noise Noise Noise

One Two
One Two three four
Noise noise noise
Smokin weed, smokin weed
Drinkin beers, beers, beers
Rollin fatties, smokin blunts
Who smokes the blunts? We smoke the blunts
Rollin blunts + smokin em
15 bucks little man put that shit in my hand,
if that money doesn't show, you owe me, owe me,
owe me, oh, my jungle love, oh ee, oh ee, oh ee, oh

– If you get it great ♥, if not its the song they are singing in the begaining of Jay + Silent Bob Strike Back one of Kevin Smith's movies, its like my favorite, along with his others Chasing Amy, Mallrats, Dogma, Clerks, + Clerks 2. I love Kevin Smith, especially with Jason Mewes, they are just so perfect.

Ok, rambling sorry, agian have a fabulous day + a long, beatiful, joyful, funfilled life. ☺ ♥

Oh, and I just realized I was suppost to write something about me or my story. Well I havn't really got a story, I'm boring, all I really do is sit in my room when I get home from school. I watch way to much tv, I'm 15 and I'm going to be 16 in December, I'm currently in 10th grade. I'm somewhat fucked up in the brain. Not in like a phychopath way, but I do self-harm and whatnot, its not that bad, none of my cuts are really that deep. I don't have many friends, but the ones I have I cherish & love dearly, for I'm lucky to have them. I'm not the most likable person in the world, I'm mean, heartless, and never do anything for others, or so I've been told. Though I try to help everyone, I fail, alot of people will end up just getting mad at me, and all my friends get bored & leave sooner or later as well. thats ok though, cuz I get it, and they deserve a better friend then I can be, I expect it but it still hurts when it actually happens. I will go out of my way for people, but it doesn't seem to matter. Even with all my efforts I'm aware that I'm still not doing anything to help or for them at all, I do it for myself so I don't feel so bad. I'm way too big, I weigh over 200 pounds, & no matter what I do It won't go away, and its driving me insane, every time I look in the mirror I just want to cry, especially if I take my makeup off. I just really try to avoid mirrors, and scales. And I love to go shopping but I hate it at the same time cuz the stuff I like, I can't find in my size & it makes me want to just cry. I don't bother people I know about any of it, because I know its stupid and would prolly just be bothersome & annoying for them, and they would prolly leave sooner if they knew. I don't look like one to struggle, If you knew me and saw how I carry myself around people, you wouldn't think anything was ever wrong with me either. I'm not as bad as other people, so I really don't think its a problem, cuz other people have actual reasons to feel this way and I just kinda do. It started when I moved from where I had such amazing friends & was just so happy to a place where no one would ever fuckin talk to me & I'd hear them makin fun of me. I moved from there 6 months later, and now I'm here, its alot better than Big Bear but I can't shake the feeling that being there gave me. I'm also not as bad as others cuz im not really suicidal. I say not really, cuz I want to die but I can't do it, I'm too weak, it more of if I happened to get hit by a car, I wouldn't care. I always walk on the street side, you know when your walking with people and theres the person on the end, where if a car were to come it would hit them, thats where I walk at, I always move people to the inside so if one comes it would hit me instead of them. Well I'm sorry if this was just annoying or bothesome, but ya. Again have a wonderful day ☺ and don't forget that you truley are a glowing, beatiful, amazing human being. ❤

Chapter Twenty Two
"RLA"

Transcription on page 218

Elijah,

I'm mailing you to let you know you inspire me. You inspire lots of people but there's a specific reason why you inspire me. You've dedicated your life to reaching out to others. I'll be the first to tell you that it is a bittersweet thing. While you have gone through your own struggles and come out with a new perspective, there will always be a piece of your mind stuck in that old life. To heal others when you're in a perpetual healing state? That's bloody heroic. So while you give us a challenge, I give you a challenge: take every letter I send to heart and decide how you'll use it to continue healing. I found you on Tumblr so hopefully I'll know if you decide to take my challenge as seriously as I take yours.

-RLA

Chapter Twenty Three
Sam

Trigger Warning: Suicide, Self Harm, Abuse

Transcription on page 219

Your videos are amazing. They give me hope that I can live another day.

My name is Sam. I'm fifteen years old. However, things are not as... Good? As one would wish. I have been cutting myself since I was twelve. I have attempted suicide six times the past two years or so. Mainly because of abuse from an ex-boyfriend, self-hatred, verbal abuse from peers, those kinds of things. I honestly don't know why I'm writing this letter. I guess I thought you might understand.

Lately, my depression has gotten worse for no reason. My cutting got worse, my suicidal thoughts worsened as well. But I stumbled across your blog on tumblr. Your self-harm video got to me. I want to stop cutting, but I don't want to. I'm afraid of relapse because each relapse is worse than the last. I don't know what to do. It's as if I've become a slave to it, yet I'm afraid to leave it.

Anyway, if you read this, I was just saying thank you. Your videos kept me from attempting again. So... Thank you.

Best Regards,
Sam

Chapter Twenty Four
Sammi

Trigger Warning: Suicide, Self Harm

Transcription on page 220

September 15, 2012

Dear Elijah,

So today while scrolling through tumblr. i saw an insteadofcutting post: Instead of Cutting #781 watch justaskinnyboy on YouTube. 25 minutes later, here I am, sitting on my bed at 10:20pm writing you this letter.

I'm sixteen years old and I'm a junior in high school. Quite honestly, it's a frickin' miracle that I made it this far. My parents divorced when I was three because my father is a raging alcoholic (who will be getting married for the fifth time in October) and was abusive. My mom and I move(d) every two-three years so I don't have friendships that have been since first grade. Nada. My grandpa, my best friend, died six years ago, less than a month before my birthday. Smiles on my birthday? No. Tears. Since then I have developed severe depression, have self-harmed and have attempted suicide multiple times.

I was able to keep my cutting a secret until last year, I finally broke down and told my two best friends who then used force to drag me into our guidance counselor's office. After showing the counselor my wrist, she told my mother. My mother's reaction? Screaming when I asked to see an outside-of-school counselor and only speaking to me when absolutely necessary. It's a really good thing she found out in November because I wasn't allowed to use a disposable razor until February. Thank God for electric razors. But when she fought me by taking the razors, I walked to the drug store on Main Street and bought a bag. I can now dismantle a disposable razor in under 3 minutes. The cuts started getting longer, deeper and fewer days were in between when I would do it.

oops; I've been seeing a therapist every other week for almost a year now and I was eight months clean before relapsing. *applause for me* Dude omg! I forgot! My name is Sam. Kcool. My mom is always so interested in what I talk about during my sessions, but never about why I do what I do. It almost makes me feel like she doesn't care.

I have three really awesome friends that I've told my story to: Jake, Jess, Ramón. Jake's known the longest. He's helped me find a more positive way to deal with my emotions, but it only works sometimes. I made a wall of mini drawings/doodles that are positive. Jess has had multiple friends commit suicide so when I get those feelings I call her, or I write my letter and give it to her the next day. Ramón is the easiest to talk to because I tell him absolutely everything that goes on in my head. Today I asked him if school buses have penises. I actually just got off of the phone with him because thinking about all of this is a huge trigger. The worst part is the best way I know to keep from crying is to cut. Viscious cycle i know.

→ there's more.

" july 24, 2012.
dear journal,
So now i'm ready to fucking kill myself. i feel judged and misunderstood. i feel alone and helpless. i feel lost. i can't do this. I can't live like this for the rest of my life. with the state/mood I'm in tonight I'll be lucky if I make it to Saturday without cutting myself. Are we having fun yet?
-S"

i feel like that all the time and I absolutely hate it. Your videos make me feel like there is hope. I wish I could put into words how much I needed that today.

I'm enclosing my latest suicide note because it has been sitting on my nightstand. waiting. i'm also putting two of my blades[9] in here. It's a start... there are more but now I have less. (if that made sense) But wait! There's more. The square picture I keep over my bed on my ceiling, right about my poster that I made that says "love is louder than the pressure to be perfect." the other two are from my inspiration wall. I want you to have them as a reminder of how much you've inspired me to recover.

Thank you so much. I love you.

- Sammi ♡

wait! thank you for taking the time to read this. and if it's not too much to ask could you mail me a reply letter?

sorry i put these in weirdly... i didn't want you to hurt yourself on them

[9] To see an image of the blades mentioned in this letter, please see pg. 161

I'm doing this because I don't know what else to do. I'm trapped, slowly suffocating. If you're analyzing, or trying to remember the last conversation we had. Stop. don't stress yourself over it. I can guarantee that this wasn't your fault and I'm sorry that you have to deal with this but it's sort of too late to do anything, or at least it will be by the time you read this.

I suppose this is when I would say I'm sorry. But funny story, I'm really not. I needed to do this for myself. And if you dont agree with my decision. I don't care. Didn't when I was alive and still don't now that I killed myself. Yup. I said it. I committed suicide. I offed myself. Gave up.

I always thought that writing this note, like for real, would be hard. That I wouldn't know where to begin and I would be crying so hard you wouldn't be able to even read the whole letter. That's why I practiced on the sides of my notes all last year. I did it in class so that I would have no choice but to supress my emotions. Pretty smart if I do say so myself.

So this is it.

Bye.

-8

Chapter Twenty Five
Stacey

Trigger Warning: Suicide, Eating Disorders, Self Harm, Abuse

Transcription on page 223

My name is Stacey, I'm 18, and I'm a college freshman. I've spent the past six years dealing with major depression, self harm issues, anxiety, and "food issues". I know that you say you are nothing special, but in a sense, you are. I'm probably giving you too much credit, but, today, today you are saving my life.

Last month, I tripped. I gave in, and it got so bad, that I was contemplating taking my own life. It's hard, getting back up after six years of failure. It gets harder every time I try again, because I'm so used to failing, so I stopped believing in myself. It's hard living in a house parents say I just need to grow up, who don't listen, who won't even try to understand. When you're living in a world full of unforgiving faces, and when you are dealt one shitty situation after another, it becomes hard to even think about being happy again.

I'm not going to spill my story to you, I don't think it's right, putting that on you. But, your words, truly keep me going. I'll wake up in a dark place, and I'll just load one of your videos for some kind words, so I can actually get out of bed that day. Some days are harder than others, but knowing that someone out there understands, makes it a little easier.

So, today, everything changes. I am reaching out to anyone who will listen. I am taking the first step, for the billionth time, and I am trying to see things in a different perspective. You know, I didn't think I was ever going able to say that, that I am going to try again. But you, and your words, and your messages, has given me a new hope. Seeing you, still trying to get better, gives me a little strength, because if you can do it, then so can I.

Elijah, Thank you. I am taking The first step. I want to get better. So take them, the blades[10], That have hurt me countless times, tiny as they may be, they have left scars that will never fade, caused pain I Thought I deserved, for things I couldn't control. I don't need Them anymore. I'm not saying that I will never hurt myself again, but this is The first step in order to get there, because I deserve better than This.

I'll end up writing again, probably to give an update, even if you don't remember me, It would be nice to let you know.

Thank you so much, Elijah. I wish you all The best, because you deserve happiness.

Stay Strong..

<3, Stacey

[10] To see an image of the blades mentioned in this letter, please see pg. 161

So i've been wanting to tell someone my story for awhile, but i've just been too scared. But I need to tell my story, I need to tell someone before it kills me. So, here it goes. It might be a little jumpy, but i'm just typing as I remember things.

I was 12, when he raped me. 12. In that moment I was forced to grow up.

I never told anyone what happened, and I really haven't until now. It's been six years, and I still feel that twang of pain when I'm remember what happened. I still blame myself on a daily basis. Even though I know it wasn't my fault, I still blame myself.

My self-hate...along with the low self-esteem...made me sink...into this pit. I quickly became depressed.

I was 13 when I put a blade to my wrist. Never deep enough for stiches, just deep enough to feel the pain. It was my punishment, for everything. Got a bad grade? Cut. Got yelled at? Cut. Didn't live up to my friends/parents expectations? Cut.

I was 14 when high school started. I didn't really have any friends, and I wouldn't really let myself open up to anyone. I was lumped in as an outcast, an emo, a freak. Cutting wasn't punishment anymore. It was the only way I could feel anything, because feeling pain was better than feeling nothing.

I was 15, straight A student, still depressed, still harming myself, it was at that point, when people started to say "Hey, have you gained weight?" I became super self conscious about my weight, and my eating habits have been poor ever since.

I was 16, straight B student, a couple friends who knew my secrets, but I could never really let anyone in.

I was 17, a C or D student, even in my honors classes; my best friend was in a coma, a close family friend died. A couple close friends tried to kill themselves. I was made fun of for my scars, for being different. I was in the counselor's office on and off for that entire year, not willingly, but because I was reported by friensd who were worried I was going to hurt myself.

Along with the depression, and the self-harm, and other issues, I also sleep. I was exhausted, but I physically could not sleep, and when I did it was because I would collapse from exhaustion. My sleeping is still so unpredictable, I can go for days on nothing but a couple hours, or I can sleep for 12+ at a time.

I was getting worse, and worse, and no one even noticed. I would lock myself in my room for days...crying, sleeping, staring at the wall. I ignored everyone and everything, my friends abandoned me. I had completely secluded myself from the world.

I would shred my skin until there was nowhere left to cut. I was numb anyway, it's not like it mattered. I would stand in front of my mirror, pulling at my skin, at my fat, hoping it would go away. I wasn't good enough for anyone..

When I would leave my room, I would be yelled at. I was a bitch, or fat, worthless, ugly, a failure, a disappointment, the problem child. What kind of parents would call their daughter names? Mine, they never tried to understand. They didn't want to acknowledge that something else was wrong with me. They refused to see what was wrong. Even when school would call home worried, they just turned the other way. It hurts knowing that they didn't even care enough to help me. They still tell me to "grow up" and "get over it, your not sad, just be happy." It's crazy, that everyone else in my family has a mental disorder, but it's not ok for me to not be ok.

During this, I had been dating someone for about 4 years. He would always poke at me, and tell me how "squishy" I was (like I wasn't worried about my weight enough), he never resorted to calling me fat, but the thought was always there. Even though he had depression and self harmed, he would always make fun of me for it. "hey what are those? Oh fresh cuts, your such a freak" "Oh what..you 'depression' is really bad today, so?" When he did get tired of me, he would leave, and I would beg him to come back. He would, but only if he had no one else to screw with. Eventually, he convinced me that I didn't need anyone else but him, that he could save me, and that I would never find anyone else. I eventually lost all of my friends, and I ended up only having him. He wasn't always a horrible person, but it was all the bad times that still stand out.

I never really knew how emotionally abusive, or what he had done to me, until he finally decided he was done with me. We had gotten engaged, and then he cheated on me, and basically said I was nothing to him. He said that she was better, and smarter, and she loved him more, and that she was "normal".

After he left, he took my oxygen with me. I had no one, and didn't want to live anymore, and in February of 2012 I tried to kill myself. Amazingly, I woke up, in my own bed...I hadn't done enough…I've never told anyone..

Even though I almost failed senior year, I miraculously made it through high school. I thought, that everything was going to be better..

Seven months of recovery happened after my attempt, but at the beginning of August, I slipped again...

I don't really know what happened..everything just got so out of control, my life went to hell, and I had no control over it.

I had to quit my dream college, because I just was so afraid of what I might do to myself, I was afraid of everything.

Anxiety ran rampant, my depression got worse..there are more scars..but I got back up..determined to fight again…

Only a month later, I relapsed, hard.

At the beginning of September, the man that ruined my life came back into town, and all of the memories came rushing back.

No eating, no sleeping, I left more scars on my body, they'll never fade away.

I discovered you shortly after he came back. I wrote you a letter, and sent you my blades, and said that I was better than self harm. Some nights, when i'm on the edge, I just listen to your videos for words of wisdom.

I aquired more blades half way through November, and I must admit that I have used them, but I have been working up the courage to send them to you, and I guess today I am. All of them, every, single, one. And this time I am promising you that I will never hurt myself again.

It's amazing, that in the past six years, I've never been hospitalized, I've never been sent to treatment. I saw a psychologist up until right after I was diagnosed with depression and anxiety, but then stopped seeing them, because my mother stopped believing me, and therapy. I was on medication for a short time, but I haven't been in years.

I'm 18, a third of my life has been hell. It still is, and every day is a constant struggle between life and death. It always will be. But I'm trying.

I have recently connected with an old friend from high school. He graduated the year before I did, and we lost touch. We are actually dating now :) He is suprisingly understanding, but I guess that's due to the fact that we share the same disorders, we support each other. It's the best feeling, knowing that after everything, there's still someone out there who won't leave, but I guess you know about that.

I haven't stood up to my mother yet, her verbal and emotional abuse still brings me to tears on a daily basis, but I'm hoping to move out with a friend later this year.

I also went back to college, and I'm working on my nursing degree.

The world is full of darkness; it's hard to forget the bad things that happen in the past, but in order to move forward, you have to forget, no matter how difficult.

I've met some amazing people in the past few months, I have a new support system. I really hope to meet them all one day.

I have no regrets, you would think that I would, but I don't. Everything that that has happened has made me who I am today. My story isn't over yet, it's a work in progress, I have recently been given the opportunity to move forward. I'm not going to stop this time. I'm not going to look back. It's time for me to be happy. It's time for me to beat this.

The Tools

In addition to the letters sent in, a handful of individuals also included the things which they had used to hurt themselves. Giving up these 'tools' was a way to take a step forward in their recovery and say "these won't hurt me anymore."

When I open a letter and I find a razor blade or box cutter taped to the letter, it is one of the most humbling experiences I have ever had. To understand the significance of receiving someone else's tools, one must understand the fact that self harm is an addiction. Just like alcohol, smoking, or drugs, the individual is very attached to the object which feeds their addiction.

Trigger Warning: The following images are pictures of the actual items sent in by each person. If razors/blades or other self harm related tools are triggering for you, please skip to page 167

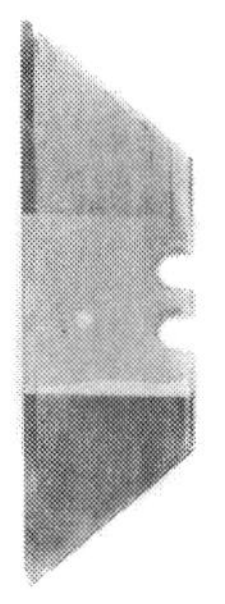

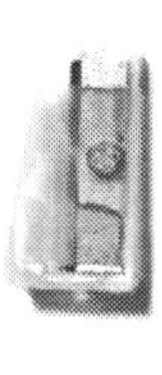

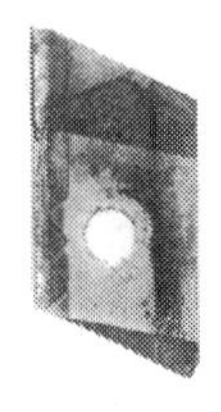

Jacklyn - Page 16

2 Box cutter blades
1 Pencil sharpener

Anna - Page 41

2 Shaver blades
1 Box cutter blade
1 Pencil sharpener blade

Ellen - Page 53

10 Box cutter blades

Grace - Page 71

4 Bobby pins
2 Pencil sharpener blades
1 Safety pin
1 Paperclip

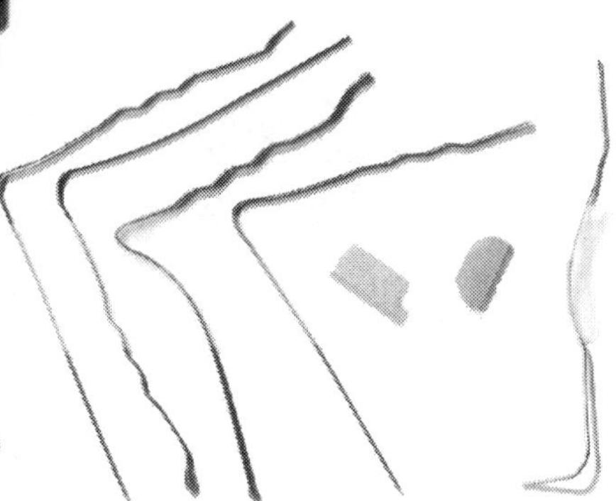

Hilary - Page 77

1 Hobby knife blade

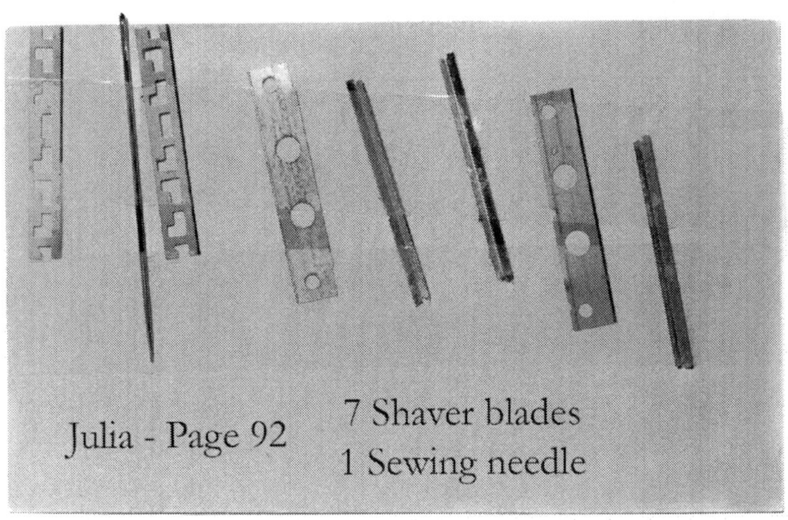

Julia - Page 92
7 Shaver blades
1 Sewing needle

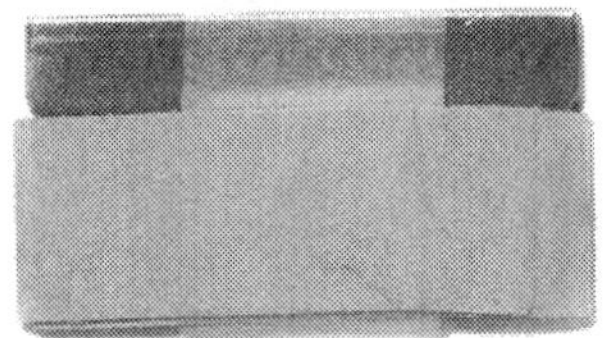

"K" - Page 100

1 Box cutter blade

Sammi - Page 147

1 Shaver blade
1 Hobby knife blade

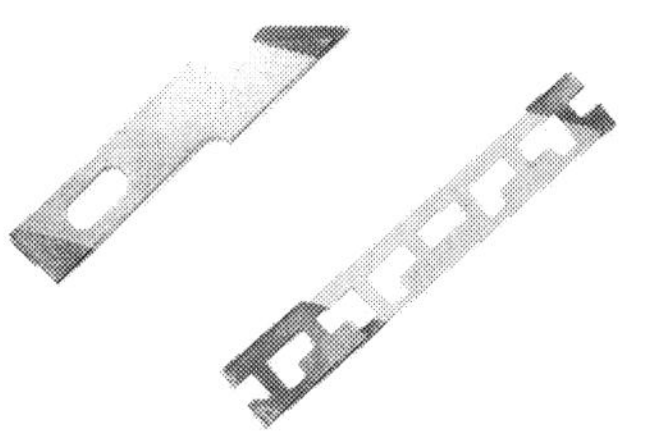

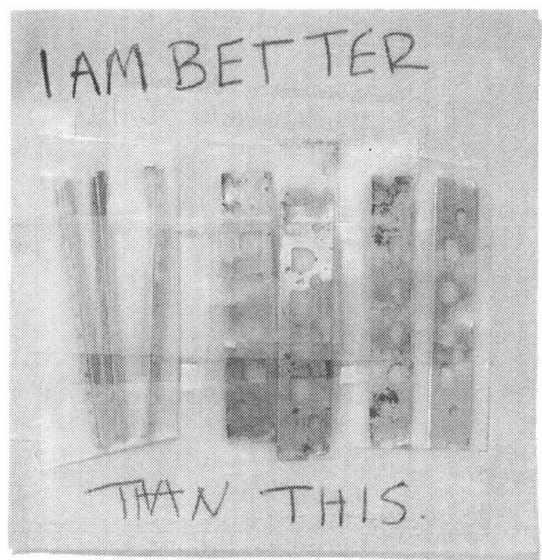

Stacey - Page 153

10 Shaver blades
6 Box cutter blades

Even the best fall down sometimes.

I'm not done fighting yet.

Part Two

~

What Now?

Butterfly Letters Experience

Butterfly Letters is more than just a book. Butterfly letters is a point of connection, a place where people can hear and be heard. We want to create a safe place where an individual's story can be appreciated and a place where everyone can know that they're not alone in the struggles they face on this great big planet of ours.

The first part of doing this is creating this book series, *The Butterfly Letters*, as a kind of catalyst for sharing the stories we have while encouraging people to send in their own. We hope that through sharing the 25 stories in this first book we will create a spark of hope and excitement in our readers. A spark that could potentially ignite a fire of connection through which many people will be touched in life-changing ways.

The second part of doing this is through the blog we have created where we will post scans all of the letters we receive. Our blog will be a place where anyone can come and read the letters we receive. Perhaps they will find one story that really resonates with them and they will comment with a snippet of their own story, adding to the kind of "conversation" of the letter. Maybe they will even send in their own letter to be read and commented on as well. And by doing so, there is a continual stream of stories to be shared and experienced.

Our desire is that with these two large steps together in harmony, we can create and sustain that special place where everyone has an outlet to which they know their story will be heard, and also they can read and relate to other stories much like theirs.

Send Us Your Butterfly Letter

If you would like to make your own contribution to the Butterfly Letter collection, here are some guidelines/suggestions on how you can go about doing that in the best way possible:

Do:

Be genuine.
An honest and vulnerable letter is one that will always make an impact.
Tell your story.
Anyone can write a fiction novel, but your story is unique; it's you!
Make a conversation.
Ask questions in your letter, give people something to talk about.
Balance it out.
Be careful not to only focus on bad stuff, be sure to mention good things too!
Take your time.
You don't have to rush to get your letter sent in, there's always time!

Do not:

Lie or exaggerate.
Your story is special enough, there's no need to be dishonest.
Be hateful or disrespectful.
Even if it's true, being negative won't help anyone.
Include personal information.
While we do think that your identity is significant, we also value your privacy and prefer to keep only the first names of individuals on the letters.
Write in lots of colors.
It's happened before, and sadly rainbow colors are hard to read.
Advertise/promote.
There is a time and a place, and this is not the time or the place.

Once you've finished your letter, you can mail it to:

Butterfly Letters
PO Box 1211
Burnsville, MN 55337
United States

By default, all letters we receive will be posted onto the blog. However, if a letter breaks one or more of our guidelines of what not to include, we reserve the right to not post that letter if we consider it to be inappropriate or insensitive. By sending a letter to the address above you are agreeing to the terms and conditions set in our disclaimer (see page 6 for details.) Sending a letter does not guarantee it will be included in an edition of *The Butterfly Letters.*

Index of Transcriptions

Chapter One — Jacklyn

Dear Elijah,

Thank you! Thank you so so so much. Really thank you because of what you did last night, you didn't have to but you did, so thank you. Last night you made me realize something. You made me realize that if I really try hard enough I don't need to cut. I now know that.

So you are probably wondering who this is, unless you figured it out already because you are super smart. It is like 3 am and I'll probably go run in an hour or so, but I would figure you know now. Well I figured maybe I would, right now, say thank you & tell you how much last night meant. I know you won't say it but I know you would have much rather have talked to Danielle than me last night or slept or done something much more productive than talk to me so thank you. It is greatly appreciated that someone in Minnesota cares about someone so insignificant like me. So thank you.

Eventually I'll mail you the blade. I will try. I don't really know cause I am extremely dependent on it, but I'll try everyday this summer if I make it through to send you it. I promise, scratch that pinky promise.

I'm going to force myself now to when I walk to the mailbox to send this but… we will see what happens.

I hope to make you happy. Take care of yourself.

Love,
Jacklyn

Dear Elijah,

Thank you for everything! Really it means so much to me, you don't even know. Seriously. I think, well actually know, you are the first person to really care in a long time. That means a lot because don't even know me but are willing to do that. So THANK YOU.

I am sending you my last two blades. I promise they are my last two. I promise you that I will try and stay clean and safe. I promise you I will try not to self harm anymore because it means so much to you. So if that is what makes you happy and will make you keep helping people than it is truly worth it. I just want to say: You were right. You were right when you said I couldn't control it. You were and I am sorry I didn't listen.

I don't know how much the next page is going to mean to you. But let me explain something. Remember when I said starting July I would never bother you again? Well… I planned something. I couldn't tell you. Why? Either:

You would be crushed and blame yourself

You would have tried to talk me away from it

A mix of both a & b.

So I am sorry. I never did what I planned. I mean yes Saturday night I cut but I stopped myself from going to far. But there is one thing I learned from your story. That is: If Elijah can make it than so can I so thank you for that. Elijah, I am giving you the note to show you how much I am going to try. Okay?

Seriously, you are such an amazing person.

You affect so many people and that is such a great thing. I really wish more people were like you. So thank you.

Honestly I am really scared to not have any blades this summer. My goal is to get through this summer. According to you I can do this but according to myself I don't know if I can. I don't want to be a disappointment or bother so I doubt I will really talk to you. I am sorry I just can't risk bothering or hurting you. If I do, I will never forgive myself.

Anyways enjoy your summer and keep doing what you are doing. I hope you and Danielle go far. Good luck in all you do.

Love,
Jacklyn

Whoever finds this or me I am sorry but this had to be done. The constant bullying inside of school, outside of school, online it was everywhere. But thing that drove me to this was my best friend telling me to kill myself. So you know what he said that along with others who told me they'd help so you know no one will notice or care. So I am sorry to whoever finds this. Don't feel bad nor feel like its your fault. Please don't follow. You are important.

I love you.

Jacklyn.

Elijah,

This is probably one of the hardest things I will ever have to write. It shouldn't be but it is and I really wish it wasn't. I cannot promise that this letter will be entirely good, bad, happy, sad, etc. because it is a mix of many emotions. I think after a few scraps of letters on loose leaf I realized I should type it, so I don't kill any more trees! I finally know exactly how I need to get across my message and I also think that I am writing this just because I want someone who I trust to know these things because honestly it isn't getting anywhere.

Anyways do you mind if I tell you a little story? So you can get why I am feeling the way I am. If you don't want to hear this story you don't have to you can just skip down to the exclamation point in the beginning of the paragraph. Okay so here it goes the story. There was this girl, her name was Jackie. Jackie was the girl who wanted to be friends with everyone even if they were the meanest people; she wanted and was their friend. Anyways, as Jackie went into kindergarten she began getting nicknames and being teased for many things. Well it's just kids being kids right? WRONG. Jackie went on to first grade. New school = new friends. She immediately became friends with Debra. Well Debra and her friends immediately clicked with Jackie. But the bullying began. She would be teased for everything. Her weight, the way she wore her hair, because she danced, anything and everything. Well it continued but eventually fifth grade came. Jackie's dad died suddenly. Jackie's school called all the parents in her grade so all the kids knew. They were all her friend. They all went to the wake and the funeral and were her friends for now. But a month later, guess what happened? She was being bullied even worse. That summer she got "tripped" to see her fall. She ended up spraining her knee, breaking her wrist and three fingers, chipping her tooth, and breaking her nose. Just to see her fall. Sixth grade they all apologized but the thing is they apologized because Jackie went to the school psychologist weekly to get over her dad and her sixth grade teacher told her that bullying was going on but he needed her to intervene with him. So she did. Problem fixed right? WRONG. Seventh grade = new school = no problems. WRONG. Shoes thrown off the bus, books thrown out the window, cupcakes thrown at her, being dragged on the bus floor by her backpack. It settled down. Freshman year death threats started and that's when I stopped eating and started burning. I stopped. My best friend wanted to kill me for it. So anyways her bra got unhooked in homeroom, her desk flipped, hair was cut, and she got stabbed with a compass (thing for drawing circles).

Sophomore year was same thing. Junior year within the first month of school she was told to kill herself, that they would help her kill herself, she was a slut, whore, bitch, whale, she was told in front of the whole cafeteria that an 8th grader would bang her on the bus and many other things. Well her friend Sam found out. She made her tell someone and it "stopped". December came around. She was being told she was a home wrecker, suicidal, purposely killing herself and starving herself. Then in February she was grabbed and bled by a guy who was her "friend", the same guy saying those things. She told the dean well he lied. He was supposed to get suspended he got out of it. But it didn't stop there. The last day of school Jackie checked the review group to wish all a happy summer. Someone posted crap about her friend Sam. She immediately went to stick up for her. It ended on Jackie though. It ended with "Jackie if you really want to get serious why don't you get your fat ass off Facebook and hit the elliptical". That drove Jackie to cutting. That also drove her to restricting.

! Nice story right? That Jackie is me. I am so scared to start school on Tuesday you don't understand. If it happens again this year I can't even imagine what will happen. I can't and the thing is the suspension from the kids on the bus was only for junior year that means... they can be on the bus this year. I can't deal with this but I made a promise to myself. If it happens, I tell NO ONE. Why? I don't want to be seen as the problem girl. I can't.

I am sorry lately for cutting. I am sorry for being the fuck up. I am sorry. Lately it's too much. I need help. I know that but the thing is I am scared to ask for it. I know I said I would tell a counselor but... I cant he already thinks I am unable to handle stuff from junior year I can't let him know I am doing this I look up to him I cant. I wish I could though. I wish I wasn't such a chicken. I feel like I might take my life.

I know I should send you my blades again and I know that you will probably tell me to but I can't and there is a good reason behind it. I feel like I put the pressure on myself to quit. I mess up under pressure. Then I get mad at myself because I feel like I made empty promises to you when I sent them because I just fail constantly. Like, I promised but then cut and mess up and become a liar and that hurts because I don't want you to feel that from anyone especially me because I know how much it hurts.

I don't know I just wish my life was worse so that I actually had a reason for being depressed and not just am depressed. I just wish I had a plausible reason to cut. I feel like I don't. I feel like hating me isn't a good enough reason. I feel like being overwhelmed isn't a good enough reason. I just wish I had a better reason to justify it all but I don't and that's the thing no one would believe the "happy" girl does this. They would think it's some crazy messed up joke. I just wish it was. I wish it was a joke and not reality. I wish this wasn't what I got myself into.

My mom doesn't know that since I have been driving with my license that as soon as she lets me on my own I don't think I can because I know one day something will happen and that I will get too upset and that I will just push myself over the edge and I will kill myself with success.

I feel myself pushing away my friends and it scares me. I have isolated and I am scared that I am seeing the signs of me being so close to suicide. I really am scared but then again I think it is better. I am out of everyone's way of life. Everyone can be much happier. I mean at the beginning no but later on yes.

Like tonight I was given the ultimatum by a friend to choose if I want the friendship or if I want it to be done. All because I distanced. It's not fair. I wish he could see how much I am struggling but he wouldn't even understand if anyone tried telling him. So now I can't really push him away when I am overwhelmed because he will end the friendship and I hate that because I know if I don't keep reminding myself not to no matter how scared and overwhelmed I get, I can't because I will lose him.

I don't know I just figured someone should know. Instead of me keeping it all bottled inside. Anyways, take care of yourself. Congrats on your relationship. I wish you well. Remember I love and care about you.

Sorry,

Jacklyn

P.S. When I finish something I am going to have to email it to you because I think you deserve to read it☺

Chapter Two — "A."

Dear Elijah,

I hope you can help me. I am not anorexic or bulimic (although my sister and ex both suffered from anorexia). I have never cut into my body. All of my scars are from surgery. Here's the kicker, though: I believe myself to have Dissociative Identity Disorder, with a current total of 15 different identities, or "alters". I am currently seeking diagnosis, but have encountered reluctance from multiple therapists, since I appear to function so well in daily life. I am reaching out to you because I need someone to talk to. You seem like such a wise, kind and caring soul. I couldn't not reach out to you. Yesterday in therapy, I asked my therapist if I could let my alters out in therapy. She discouraged me; said it would be "a step backwards". I was hurt, discouraged that she would advise against expressing myself. All the parts inside me need to be recognized, and cared for. I was hoping the laters that wanted to could write to you, Elijah.

I wish I could include my tools for self-injury, but my most dangerous tool is the self-hate I carry inside myself.

I only included my first initial on the envelope, because I have a unique name and do not wish for my identity to be revealed publicly.

Dear Elijah,

I hate being fat. I wish I was thin. I wish I had a gap between my thighs, not just because of the way it looks, but because of the way it feels. I can't wear skirts because I get a painful rash between my thighs. I am hot all the time, and I sweat after minimal exertion. I am 20 years old, but I have to wear granny bras because they don't make cute bras in my size. I can't run.

I wish I was thin so I could fit clothes from forever 21. I wish I was thin so I will be respected. I wish I was thin, so I don't have to be one of the "fat girls". I wish I was thin so my mom would stop making comments on what I eat. I wish I was thin so I could curl up into a tiny fetal ball and hide. I wish I was thin so I could run fast, and far.

It makes me so sad to hate my body; my perfectly functioning body. My body that has kept me alive all these years, and done me no wrong. My body that has survived surgery, meningitis and a car accident. It's not my body's fault, it's mine. I let this happen, and I don't know how to undo it. I don't even know where to start.

Please help,

-Rinata

Chapter Three — Alice

Dear Elijah,

I've never written to someone I don't know and have never met. And honestly I'm not really sure what to say. But I've rewritten this letter 3 times wanting it to look perfect, but I realize it's not going to be perfect. Nothing is but that doesn't mean it's terrible.

I first found out about you, was by my friend. I was on tumblr and I saw what my friend wrote about you. It was "Also, a person who inspired me is Elijah. I'm sending him my blades and my story on Monday." I asked her who you were and went to your tumblr page. I read your story and thought it was incredible and the first video I watched was the one with you and Lauren about your favorite memories and it was your 2 month anniversary. It was the cutest thing ever. Then my friend sent me the one on self harming and it brought me to tears. I loved it. Videos like those, I've never cried when I watched them.

That video was amazing and it touched me. It was amazing for someone to say something that I feel so much of the time. You and Lauren said all the things I'm scared to say to anyone else but inside I'm screaming it silently. I loved feeling not alone

Knowing someone understands and my favorite thing you two said was "things will get better. It can get better, it does get better. Maybe not tomorrow, maybe not next week, maybe not for a year, but things will get better." Because anytime someone has said that to me or said "it will be okay" I've never fully believed them 100%. But those 3 sentences made me believe 100%.

There's times when I've been at my total worst and have cried out for help silently but have been terrified of the outcome and result. I see that I really am not alone, there are others that are the same as me.

I was going to cut tonight but I didn't and it's thanks to you, Lauren, and my friend. Thank you for saving me tonight, there will probably be more to come but I'll just watch the video and know I'm not alone. Sadly, I'm not strong enough for you're challenge – to send you my blades but I can part with them tonight and that they'll be nowhere near my skin to make a mark. I want to get better and this seems to be a first good small step. Thank you again, so much.

Chapter Four — Ana Beatrice

May 13th, 2012

Hey,

It's 5:30 a.m. on a Sunday and I didn't sleep at all. I'm writing you a letter, don't know why, but I'm doing anyway. Maybe I want to have one of those friendships by letter that people used to have but I think that on these letters the person talked about their lives and I'm not gonna do that, that's not my type of letter. Truth be told I don't really have a type of letter, besides may be debts. I really don't know what type of letter is that, but probably not a "fan" mail either, 'cause I'm not gonna say how amazing you and your blog are, you already knows that)If you don't I'm opening an exception in these parentheses: You are fucking amazing, you're handsome, smart, artistic, have the perfect eyes, a curly golden hair which is the cutest thing I ever saw and the most important you're trying to help the others. You're the guy of my dreams if you want to marry just call me I'm free anytime lol), anyways I really don't know what this letter is about, maybe it is just some random babbling of a insomniac girl. Another thing I'm really sorry about my grammar mistakes, I checked this a couple of times but you know, there's always something that slips away.

The envelope contains some other stuff, 'cause when I wrote this on Sunday I wrote it a short story, actually I wrote the story first and I thought about sending you a photo too. Then I got carried away during the week and end up doing a draw and buying some bracelets to you, so I'm gonna tell you about the stuff that I'm sending you. The short story that I wrote It is in portuguese, and I really think it's

Better this way. I actually write most of my stories in English but for some reason this one come to me in portugese. So I propose you that it stay that way, that you don't try to translate on does online translations, 'cause let's be honest my story it's not that good and probably gonna get a lot worse if translated on those. But if you know someone that knows portugese than that person can translate to you. So it's a deal? Okay, I know you cannot really answer that and you can do whatever you want with the story but I really do hope that you do as I'm asking. Some other thing about the short, please that good care of her, it is the only cop that

I have and you know may be someday when I'm gonna be like Oprah famous you can sell that on ebay :)

I'm sending you a photo which is a monument somewhat famous, the Christ. Okay I know my photo is not wonderful or anything and the quality is pretty bad but I'm not asking you to review or anything and I like this photo a lot. It was taken about a month ago and I really feel like sending to you so you can get to know a bit more about Rio de Janeiro, 'cause I really love this city. And I really want everybody to love too, 'cause my city is wonderful, so beautiful, and I feel like sometimes people let pass it by. There's so much beauty, wonderful places that are not touristic spots and people that live in the city don't really care about or don't see the beauty. Anways you should come visit something. I would love to welcome you here. Now about the draw, I did that inspired on the Coldplay song Fix You, which I'm kind obsessed for the past three months. I like a lot the original but I truly love the Boyce Avenue version (they made a cover of What Makes You Beautiful – One Direction and it's amazing, and I'm not really fangirl of OD, okay I am but they're brits

There's not how to not love them). So that's about it of the draw, I really appreciate drawing but I'm not really talented so I guess my art is mail :) Okay not really, on high school I was forced to study technical draw, so I know a bit about perspective and unfortunately a lot about hospital sectors so if you need to organize a floorplan of a hospital according to the sector I'm here for you :) Okay, last but not least there are the bracelets, so they come with some words in portuguese, they had wrote in English but I thought portuguese would be cute. So let me tell you the meanings of the world. Amor = love; borriso = smile; felicidade = happiness; esperanza = hope; Don't worry I'm not fooling about the meaning, you can check it on google. Of, if you I can teach you how to say the words :)

So right now it is about 6:30 a.m. and soon the people will be celebrating mother's day and the only thing I can think is about the people who don't have what to celebrate or how to celebrate. I really would like to think that today all the people are happy but I know the world doesn't work like that. That our society make lots of people cry from sadness, from hungry, from pain, from exploitation. There a numerous of people miserable physically, mentally, and you and I know what it's like to suffer and be mentally miserable. You know I really try to help others, I do think this is my obligation as a citizen, I work voluntarily with the kids, and I really try to treat everyone with respect, as equal. 'Cause after all we are equals independent of our social status, money or appearance. But I just feel like it what I do is nothing compared to the grand picture, I feel really powerless. I'm a communist, more like a marxist and I really try to fight for equality, fight politically (before you get scared I'm must say relax, I don't eat children, at least not everyday, they are really hard to cook LOL) but I just feel like it's nothing sometimes. I really like children I always bonded with them and I dream of adopting since I was 10 or 11, and it really brakes my heart that some kids don't have parents, don't have a home, are being abused and we act like it's not our problem. I just ask myself if I'm not part of these children's problems, I close my eyes for these children like most of us. I just wish I was zillionaire and could take the children that are hurt, that cry. I really think it would be better if I was feeling this pain, and they were happy.

Okay I wrote more than I planned about this. I can't help it, I just get carried away. I just think that we as collectively should stand up, 'cause we don't have to always be like that, we can be a better society. Society it's this way 'cause we build this way, we can rebuild as our wish. We don't have to be oppressed, we don't have to deal with the crap that other people put us through, we can stand up, we can occupy. And I guess in a way it's what you are doing with your blog, you are telling people to not be slaves of others, of this sickness, that we can help each other overcome our illness, that mental illness lots of times is overlooked and it is as serious as any disease. I truly admire your blog. Once again I got a bit carried away, it's a normal thing for me but usually I'm speaking not writing. I'm aquarius so it's normal. Anyways don't know if you believe in astrology. I sort of do and sort of don't. I try to be open-minded but sometimes astrology tell some nonsense.

Again I'm sorry that I wrote so much and the end is a bit messy. I like to say thank you if you actually had the patience to read the whole letter, 'cause I know some parts are pretty boring, but anyways most of the letter I wrote without haven't slept at al so I guess I have an excuse. Hope you liked the letter. Any questions about my calligraphy can be on facebook LOL.

Oh, I realize that I didn't say my name or anything. I'm Ana Beatrice, 18 years old, Rio de Janeiro Brazil and that's it I think.

Bye Sweetie

Chapter Five — Anna

Here Are My Blades, All of them.

It's time to recover.

I can do this. I will do this.

For my daughter and, soon to be here, Son.

Thanks for the hope

Xoxo,

Anna

P.S. I wrapped them in tape for safety.

Chapter Six— Courtney

Hope you can read my handwriting

Dear Elijah,

Whenever I get mail it makes me feel happy and loved which is why I decided to send you some. You've made a difference in the world, don't ever forget it. I hope to meet you someday because you're such a sweet and understanding guy and that shows through your videos and blogs.

I wanted to share some of my story with you. A year ago I started my first year of college. I was my first time leaving Delaware and being far away from my family. When I'm at school I only see my family every month or two.

I'm usually a shy person but I tried to be more friendly last year. I tried to be friends with lots of different people but nobody liked me. Even my roommate moved in with someone else leaving me in a dorm by myself. I felt so alone. In addition to that my grades weren't good and I didn't make the colorguard team. All of these things seemed to send me the message "You're not good enough," and "You don't deserve to be happy." My cutting to worse, especially when I tried going to the counseling office. It just made things so much worse. I thought that I couldn't get better on my own but maybe I can.

I'm now starting my second year in college and I hope that this one will be better than the first. I made one really close friend last year and we're rooming together. I joined a club with nice people and now I have someone to eat dinner with every night. I have a chance to fix my GPA so I can stay in the elementary education program.

I want to recover so I'm giving you one of my razor blades. I hope I will give you my other one someday. I've been a month without cutting which probably doesn't sound like much but it's a big deal for me. It's a start. Even thought it's been hard it's been worth it. I've been using a lot of distraction techniques but reading your blog is my favorite. You inspire me to never give up. Your blog makes me feel like I don't have to change, I'm okay the way I am.

Thank you.

Hugs from Pennsylvania,

Courtney

Chapter Seven — Eleni

26/9/2012

2:00 in the morning

Hi Elijah! ☺

This probably the 98752568th letter I am writing to you. I destroyed every one of the previous letter, beause they did not include enough words to say "Thank You". I think though that words will never be enough. Only I will ever know how much good you've done to me. And I wanted you to know that I appreciate it. A lot.

People never helped me. It's not that they didn't try. I just … dislike people. So, no matter how good someone was to me, I would always turn my back. Avoid any human connections. I still do. But you … you somehow touched me. Not right away. Besides I first met you on 9gag! When I saw that post, I never imagined that you were a person with a history like that. I would never imagine that we had things in common. At that point, I was a few months away from being 16 and I was cutting myself for the past 4 years. I had broken four bones of my body with a hammer, and I'd already tried to kill myself six times. In one word, I was "hopeless". My ED (bulimia) was at its finest and I was so close in attemting killing myself again. It was meant for that night. I had the pills, I had everything I needed. But then I saw your blog, your story. That night I stayed awake. By the morning, the pills were still inside that box and I was still alive. Breathing. Until then, I wasn't actually living. Just surviving through the days, through the events. That day, was the day my life started. I remember being 7 years old. A kid full of joy. Until some other classmates of mine called me fat. Technically my life is paused since then. I wasted 9 years of my youth, hating me. Hating everything about me. It's not fair. That was when I realized it. I started LIVING. I continued my life from the day I paused it. Of course, nothing is the same and it will never be, but I'm so happy to say that I even like myself sometimes. Before depression was home to me and happiness a place I rarely visited. And I am proud to say that today, things are the other way around. I smile. And after all those years, that smile is real and it doesn't hide any pain. I learned – with you – to express my feelings. I smile because I want to, because I feel like it, because I deserve it. I cry because bad things still happen. You taught me that not all days are gonna be good and that life has its upsides and downs. With your own special, unique, majestic, amazing way you saved me and from the bottom of my heart I thank you. Today I still have my moments. There are times when I purge what I eat. And I know that these times are going to disappearing completely (I wish, I really do). I haven't cut myself or hit myself in the last 4 MONTHS! :D

Mostly though, I am thankful that I still have my life. I am here. And after many years I am planning to stay. I wanna come to the US and study music performance. I won a piano scholarship for my two last years of High School in a private school. That will make things much easier. And I promise you that I will come at your house the first week I'll arrive at USA.

So, make sure that you will be there.

Make sure that you will keep trying, even if some days are darker than the normal. Because you are an inspiration Elijah. To SO MANY PEOPLE. Me included. And I wanted you to know that I will be there no matter what. 'Cause I care about you. More than you can understand.

And I love you.

Please never forget that.

I care, I love you, I'm here. And you? You will never ever ever ever gonna have to be alone.

Take Care

Eleni

Chapter Eight — Ellen

Hello, well now that the whole weird greeting is out of the way, I can say thank you. Although I still struggle with self harm and will for awhile. I decided to send some of them to you, razors, that is. In advance I would like to say that I'm sorry for the terrible handwriting, grammar, and some spelling. I would like to say thank you for doing what you've been doing. Also, you and your girlfriend are adorable together, hold on to her while you have her. You never know when today is the last day that you'll see her.

So, I just realized that that made absolutely no sense, sorry about that. I'm just kinda scared, like I have been for the past four years. This stupid journey that I've made myself go through. I don't think that I've ever told someone my story completely before, so bear with me if it seems completely stupid and pointless, but it's what has gotten me to this point.

I guess my story begins a year before I was born. My dad was on his way home from a date with my mom when a milk truck ran him over (he was in a small Hundai (?)). They though that he was dead until he moved his arm slightly. In that accident, he was changed forever. He made it out alive but received a closed head injury. I don't know if you know anything about head injuries but they're quite awful. Now he has an explosive side which scares the shit out of you.

Don't get me wrong I love my dad, but growing up having to be careful about what you say to your dad is a very uneasy feeling. He'd get so stressed out that he'd explode, it was absolutely terrifying. He'd hit me when he got extremely angry. I always deserved it though, I shouldn't have been near him, annoying him.

What scared me is as I was growing (sexually) I remembered things that started to scare me. That was when I realized what had happened. I don't know how long it lasted. I just know it happened enough for me to remember vivid details. Some say that my father is an idiot for doing this and letting it happen, but I personally try to forget it.

In the first grade, I lost my grandfather, my favorite person in the world. It was like I didn't have someone for me anymore. My dad, naturally, fell apart and began to explode more frequently. He would throw things, mostly fans and glass, he would pound on the walls continuously (?) until a hole had formed. I don't know if he was filled with more pride or shame in everything he had done. But after a few years, it got better… for a while.

Then in February 2005 my worst nightmare happened. My best friend was diagnosed with Luckemia (not sure if I butchered that word). For five years, I watched her lay in that hospital bed bearly hanging on as the cancer tried to take everything she had. But she won that battle, and things were ok. Until seventh grade when I was diagnosed with clinical depression.

I was always sad, so my mom immediately sent me to the good old doctor and put me on meds. A few months after my cousin and I were raped by some "friends" of hers. That night still haunts my dreams. I can still hear her screams and feel the hands all over you. That is something, I'd never wish upon anyone, ever. Then 8th grade came and everything changed. I broke down completely, lost my happy fake exterior and gained a lost, sad, depressed, lonely and scared facad. I tried to be strong, but I couldn't for very long. That was when my relationship with John and my razors began. Both would put me in the hospital and cause me neverending pain.

I was never very smart when it came people, school; I could do it, but when someone would have a problem with me, my solution was to ignore them until the problem went "away." I've lost more friends that way than anything else. Is it normal to think about your razor everyday? To reassure yourself that you can cut in just a little while? That things can get better once you cut away your sorrows. All of the memories kept coming back and I couldn't take it anymore.

On February 25, 2011, I was seconds from death. I had enough of living this hell, so I took a razor and sliced and sliced over and over until my arm didn't have any more room. But, I was still hungry for more blood. So I moved to my leg and sliced and sliced. The sight of seeing that open area slowly start to well made me feel… alive. I had sent the goodbye text and waited for my angel to take me. But all I got was a cop. A friend had called the police.

My dad found out that night that I had been cutting. I've never seen him so distraught, he started crying in the hall while the nurses took my blood pressure. It was horrifying to see my strong 6'6 dad, slide to the ground in tears. Do you know what that does to you? To you see the center, rock, of your world fall all because of you?

That day, I saw what was worth living. For a few months I was fine, two months without cutting or attempting suicide. And then it all went to shit. I guess that's how it normall goes, life sees that you're happy and it slaps you around until you give.

I no longer have thoughts (constantly) of suicide, but my cutting has become worse. It's become daily, hourly even. I've gotten to the point where I bring my razors to class, I pull over on the side of the road to relieve the pain, and I can't focus anymore: like right now. I'm in class and all I want to do is cut, hell I just did a minute ago, but it's not enough.

My friends don't understand what this is. They don't get why this is all happening and why I'm putting them through this. To be honest, I don't even know why I'm putting them in this position. I'm terrified, and what is there that I can do? I've been asking myself this question for months until I saw your videos and I knew that maybe, just maybe I could give some of them up. I can't give them all because I think I'd freak out, but I can give you some.

I'm really scared that I can't do this. I know that people have done this and that they're alright now, but I've been struggling for years. How can I give something up that hasn't left me since I got it. Be strong and don't give up like I have. I know that this is beyond stupid of me, but I don't know what to do. My mom's ready to put me in the hospital and I don't even have a door anymore. I'm only 16 and I don't want to be here right now, there has to be some solution, somewhere that can help to change all of this… crap.

It's scary that since I've gotten my license, three months ago, I've bought several, no dozens of razors. Am I the only one who has done this? Am I really that screwed up or is this normal? I don't really know how to stop this. It's like my world's crumbling down around me and I can't rebuild it.

I'm sorry for rambling and I don't expect a reply. But for kicks and giggles my email address is (omitted). It would be amazing to know that I'm not the only one who has suffered from this.

Chapter Nine — Erica

10-4-12

Dear Elijah,

I don't really know what to say to you. I feel too awkward to even start this letter in a meaningful way. That's probably not a good sign, considering I'm in a journalism class (same class as the last letter) so I should be good at writing leads and such.

I want to restart so badly, but then I'll know that I can't eve write a little letter to "some guy on the internet" (No offense. That's mostly how my sister refers to you and other tumblr people)

I guess I should start getting to the point now? I don't know how to say this. Sorry if it's just a bunch of random words and sentences. I don't own any blades. I never have. However, I have scars on my hands from about second grade. Most of them are only barely visible, but there was five on my right and three on my left that you could see better than the others. Some of the lighter scars are also on my arms. I just counted a total of seven on my arms. The ones on my hands used to be slightly more visible. About two months ago (August 9th) I made the eight scars bleed. Actually, the bleeding wasn't bad, but at least the top layer of skin was gone. They hurt to touch for about a week and a half. Sometimes, when I got mad at myself, I would pick at them to bleed again. I've let them go and am trying my hardest to let them heal. I don't think they're ever going to look like my normal skin again. So far, six of the eight have almost completely healed. There's one on the top of my right wrist and one on my left hand that still need a little bit of time.

As of last night, there's a new, much lighter scar, also on my left hand. It's slightly curved. You may think this is stupid and childish (I know I do) but I bit myself last night. I didn't bite hard enough to break skin. At the time, I wanted to so badly, but I didn't have the guts to do it. Now, I'm glad I stopped. I was just under a lot of stress and I was exhausted (on many levels) but I knew I would just be more mad at myself if I went through with it.

My point is (two paragraphs later) that I can't send you what I've used to hurt myself. Honestly, I never considered it self-harm before recently. Anyway, I can't send you fingernails or teeth or jaw. I'm the one that has something against myself, not a blade, not a knife, not safety pins, and not a flame. I don't know if you read or will read this whole thing, but thank you. You have no idea how much it means to me to actually have someone that will listen and not judge.

Thank you again,

Erica

P.S. Sorry this is so many words. It took me all of 3rd hour. But it was worth it.

Not that you care when I'm writing this…

Friday 9-28-12

9:30 A.M.

Dear Elijah,

You still haven't told me if you read my letters from July/August. I'm in class right now, trying to figure out how to get my school to invite you to speak here. I also don't know whom to talk to about it. I know that we have already established that you will eventually come, because I know you want your bracelet.

It's really bad, because I'm not even sure who my principal is. Even if I did, I wouldn't know how to confront him and say, "There's this guy on the internet who makes videos to make people feel good. He wants to speak at schools and I think we should invite him here." I'm just a little freshman, remember?

I don't know if I can talk to my friends about inviting you because they say I talk about internet people too much… and I guess they're right. They kind of tune out right when I say the word "internet".

Maybe I could try talking to a teacher but the teacher that I'm closest to is my German teacher. I don't really know what authority she has. She's one of the heads of the Freshman Class which I guess is something.

Sorry if this doesn't seem well thought out. I only just decided to write this letter. I decided to write it for two reasons. One is by means of procrastination. I really do not want to do my work right now. The other is to let you know of basically all I said on the front.

Hope to see you soon,

Erica

P.S. I could feel/see my handwriting getting progressively worse. Sorry.

P.P.S. I knew how to sign it this time! :)

Chapter Ten — Grace

Dear Elijah and Lauren.

My name is Grace, and I'm 13 years old and I live in the UK, England. I'm writing to let you know that by the end of your video, I was crying so much, more than I ever had in my life. I was touched by it, because like some of my friends (Internet Friends!) had viewed it, and we all felt like it was speaking to us. It's one of the loveliest videos I've seen addressing Self Injury. I'm so glad you included an address, because I love to able to contact people who create touching videos!

I've struggled with issues all my life, I've actually injured myself through frustration since I was around 5 years old. It started with hitting and punching, scratching and pulling my own hair. I've always been bullied, and it's impacted so much on me. I've been called nearly every name under the sun, it's safe to say. I never had much luck with friends or love either. I get really paranoid about talking about myself, because I get worried people think I'm self centred so all I'm going to say is that I'm on medication for my Bipolar II, and I suffer with psychotic symptoms when I'm having a manic episode.

People have always seen my problems as attention seeking, and when I got a diagnosis, everyone just takes pity on me. I've tried to commit suicide. It hurt everyone around me and they didn't realise how much mental pain I was in. Anyway. My pulling, punching, hitting and scratching turned to cutting. I made my first cut aged 11. The scars in the video really stuck out to me, because the depression might stop, but the scars will always remain, mental and physical.

I really can't get over how striking your video was. Honest. You and Lauren have basically explained my life. In a video. And I can't thank you enough for how inspiring you are. I don't hurt myself as much now. I have found some ways to deal with my pain, but sometimes it's too overwhelming. So I'm sending you my blades. All of them. Every single one. It's so hard for me to do, but whenever I enter a shop, to steal (yes, that's what my habit has come to) myself some blades, I'm going to think of your video. And walk out the shop, feeling happy with myself. Your video has helped me more than counseling ever has. And I thank you for that. Honestly.

Chapter Eleven — Hannah

I support the butterfly project.—I even have my own butterfly!

August 30, 2012

Dear Elijah,

Remember sassy Maddie from "Mail Time 8"? Well she's my best friend and she told me about your video. I just watched "So You Think You're Worthless?" and… It was exactly what I needed to hear. I'm starting my journey to recovery from depression, cutting, and suicidal thoughts and actions. That's why my razor was included in this. I promised Maddie I wouldn't cut again, I promised my other best friend, and now I'm promising you. Starting today, I'm going to try to be a happy girl! J And a message that, if you feel like it, I think people should know: Yeah, I know sometimes pain gets so unbearable. Please don't self-Harm. Please don't starver yourself, and PLEASE don't attempt suicide. The consequences definitely aren't worth it.

The end of the message. Thank you Elijah…

Love,

Hannah

P.S. I went from April-August being a cutter. The scars aren't worth it.

Stay Strong

Chapter Twelve — Hilary

My name is Hilary and I don't want to be anonymous anymore. I want to feel confident and I want my voice to be heard. I want to be significant. I want to matter. And I'm on my way there. No matter how long or hard it is, I promise I'll get there.

Thank you, Elijah and Lauren for posting that video on Tumblr. It may just have turned my life around. I self harm and I suffer from depression and split personaity. I wish I could send you my blades. I really wish I could! But I actually got rid of them a while back. So I'm sending you this instead. This weird piece of paper is my "inspiration." I made it as an alternative to suicide one night, and each night, I would look at it as an accomplishment. This is the night I decided to recover. I made it in early June, or late May. I did pretty well. I thought I did it.

But when school started, my parents started fighting again. My sister started to abuse me again. And I cracked. I gave in to the urge. I cut my hip on September 19. I don't regret it. Why?

Because my cut before that was on June 2. More than 100 days. I'm looking at the bright side. I didn't cut for 100 days!

I guess that's just who I am. I like to look at what I've recovered from:

- Suicidal tendencies (woohoo! I still have thoughts though)
- Anorexia (I actually got up to a healthy BMI wow!)
- Social anxiety disorder (what is there to be afraid of?

I'm only 15. I've barely lived! How can I be so sure I want to die when I haven't even been anywhere? This stupid fight isn't over until I win, and I have so many years ahead of me to make sure that's exactly what I do!

Anyways, I thought I'd explain my "inspiration" to you so you understand it.

Basically, this is a statement of "I don't care about my OCD. I'm going to make this how I want it!" Hence the random dot, fabric, paper and the badly drawn girl. This is what it means to me:

The stars:

The quote "look at the stars, look how they shine for you" was the only quote I could believe. I guess it's because I think the stars are metaphors. Each star represents 1 person who loves you, who will always , and who is willing to do anything for you. How many stars are out there? Countless…

Faith:

To be honest, I'm an Athiest, so I don't know why I put a cross as the t, but it was supposed to mean "have faith in yourself, because you can do it." Faith means that even if you fall, you'll still get back up, knowing this time you'll go longer without falling. And I need that. I really do.

Mistakes/Underestimate:

It's okay to make mistakes. We all make them. It isn't the end of the world or your life. Just a bump in the road. And do not ever underestimate people. Chances are, most of them are suffering a similar battle and who are you to question their strength.

"Here's an umbrella" "Thanks":

This is sort of in the format of a text message. Kind of like person 1 is saying to person 2, "hey, I know what you're going through. Maybe I can help?" Like person 1 is giving person 2 an umbrella for the rain. Again, metaphor.

Gold pen quote: "anything worth undoing ain't worth doing." Was the quote of my life when a boy named Jeremy bullied me nearly to death in grade 8. He tried to apologize to me after I missed a few days of school because of him. "I didn't know." "It was a joke." Were his excuses. But it's no use. Those things he said to me… They're a part of me forever now. I lost 10 months of memories because of him. I can't remember 2011 at all because I was in so much shock. I will never forget those nights he tore my life apart.

Hope over fear:

Recovery is scary. It's absolutely terrifying. But I'm getting used to it. Because the only thing stronger than fear is hope. With hope I know that against all odds, I can do it. I can recover.

Taped up blade:

This one is my favourite of them all. I used this blade to cut myself. I also used this blade to cut a piece of paper until it was so dull, it couldn't cut my skin, no matter how hard I tried. I won. I won the battle for now. So I took my useless, dull, defeated blade and I taped it to my "inspiration" like a trophy. I won that round. I killed the blade. The blade died. Its funeral. Not mine.

But the battle isn't over. I'm not anywhere near recovered. Far from it. I don't know if I'll ever get better. The scars are too deep and the voices always come back. But like I said: I'm 15, and I'm not giving up. I know it's bad that I broke my self-harm free streak, but today is day 3, and I'm trying again. This time, 150 days. I can do it. I know I can. I'm on this Earth for a reason, and I'm going to find it. I'm going to keep going. I'm going to survive. Because I am strong. Strength to me is the ability to stay alive, survive 12 years of constant bullying, qualify for the Olympics and look Jeremy in the eye and smile. He couldn't kill me. Nothing can. I'm too broken. I'm simply unfixable. Fine. It's a challenge.

And, of course, I have to thank you for giving me hope. I remember watching your video on how "skinny doesn't get you anything" and there I was, frail, off-season Hilary, weight at 90 lbs, starving. You killed my voices. Whatever they said, you were stronger. And I was able to gain the weight back and be healthy. Now I'm hovering around 110 lbs! Healthy enough.. Anyways, as I was watching your video, I was crying. I couldn't stop. Because of you, I was able to recover from anorexia. Hopefully, you can help me recover from 11 years of self-harm. (Yes, I've been self-harming since I was 4 It only got bad when I was 12) But I'm going to do it, whatever it takes. Thank you, Elijah, I can never thank you enough for saving my life.

I may just be an insignificant face in Toronto, but I have a dream and a hell of a lot of determination. I don't care how many times I fall. I will get back up. And I will not stop until an Olympic gold medal is hanging around my neck. I will thank Jeremy for telling me I can't. Because without him, I never really would have had the fight to begin with.

"Don't cry because of what you've been through. Smile, because of what you got through." – Me

"Fall down 7 times, stand up 8." – Unknown

"They tore me apart, I'm back at the start, but I guess that's better than the end." –Me

"You were given this life because you are strong enough to live." –Unknown

No matter how bad it gets, I'll always have those 100 days. My life is far from finished. It's barely getting started. I have an entire life of opportunity and an unfinished bucket list to complete. I can't wait to get out there and Live.

Thank you so much for reading all of that. I know it was long. Stay strong. I believe in you. My "inspiration" keeps me strong. I just hope it will do the same for you.

Take care,

Hilary

Chapter Thirteen — Jani

Why hello there Elijah? I guess?

So I watched the self harm video where you said to send you blades, but I realized that wouldn't do too much because while I have blades I like, when it comes down to it, anything and everything could be a weapon. This actually came right after I relapsed and have been thinking about this stuff a lot, but realistically, the blades leave the scars, but it's the stuff in your head that really hurts you. So I decided to participate by sending a letter instead. You can't tell by this shitty example, but I'm actually a terrific pen pal. I've just never written to someone I don't actually know before. Oh and I suck at socializing. So uh yeah… I think that's all of the disclaimers I have for you.

Hi. I am your dime a dozen basket case of a #foreveralone recovering anorexic. I've got a list of diagnoses a mile long (well, depending on the font size) but I don't like them because to me they're just labels that help the other PHDs understand how my head works better. So I'm not including those. Good. That's out of the way. Um. Yes. I'm a cutter. No. I don't have a clue why writing you sounded like a good idea, because I don't know what to say and tbh I wouldn't write me back anyway. I'm a ballerina, I'm a rock climber, I have a min pin named Sharky who's adorable as all get out and who's my Emotional Support Animal, uhh I don't know what else is note worthy… I got to the U of Utah majoring in Ballet and PRT (Parks Recreation & Tourism) with an emphasis in Adventure & Outdoor Programs (basically a degree in playing outside) and hopefully I'll start my 3rd major next semester which is EMS.

God only knows why I'm telling you all of this. I followed you a while back after yet another relapse when I stumbled upon one of your videos. But, I'm a really shitty follower cuz I don't stalk your blog like I probably should so I really don't know much about you except that your girlfriend is adorable and pretty. (You should pass that on)

Idk. I was a good follower for like a day and sent you a message so I'm a winner. I've now irritated you on 2 kinds of media. Yay.

So uh the purpose of this letter? I guess I could turn it into fan mail because I feel people should be praised when they do good, and you do. But really, I needed something to do to pass some time while I have so much. Suicidal ideation and without a distraction I might think of it into action so there you have it, I am using you. Hopefully you don't mind, which you shouldn't because if you don't want to read it you could always just trash it.

So uh tumblr… let's talk fandoms. Guess you could say I'm Supernatural, BtVS, Firelyf, idk I'm sure there's lots more than that, making a list was harder than I though hah in any case... Um here is shark because this is from your self harm video and apparently self injury shark is a thing.

Oh fun fact: I can't draw for beans but I usually do anyway. Are you anywhere near Duluth? One of my best friends is from there… Anywho I guess I'll let you get back to your life and the real world now. Send me a letter sometime if you ever feel like pen paling it up or need to rant or whatever

Chapter Fourteen — Jen

You my dear are an inspiration to so many people, and that includes myself. I want to tell you, I'm not afraid to tell my story anymore. And I'm starting with telling you my story, because I remember that you care. I know we've never met and probably never will, but that's okay, as long as I know there's someone out there who cares. So heres my story if you're willing to listen. I've struggled through depression and anxiety and self harm since grade five. Of course in grade five when I bruised myself on purpose, I didn't know it was self harm. All I knew was that I was upset and I needed to get away from it. In grade five I didn't even think I'd turn out like I did.

In grade six I started cutting myself. I don't remember exactly what gave me the idea to cut, but I did, and I still regret the day I decided to pick up that blade. Some guys found out what I did and they started messaging me, saying I was a freak, they called me emo. Some of them told me they'd come to school and shove a snickers bar down my throat. (Im deathly allergic to all nuts) They said theyd take care of killing me, so I didn't have too. I took the bus home in middle school, those same boys were on my bus and got off at the same stop as me. They'd walk behind me and throw rocks at my head. Last year in grade nine, things almost seemed to get better, then I relapsed. I had to go to mental health, and see a specialist… In may of last year I was admitted to the hospital. In the hospital I had two guards with me at all times. They watched my every move. They heard me cry at night. The bathrooms didn't lock and there was no shower curtain, it was like they could have come in at any moment. I wasn't allowed my worry stone, I wasn't allowed bracelets… I wasn't even allowed to wear my own underwear.

Some guys at my school started treating me like an object. I'd just broken up with my boyfriend and those guys had been annoying me, they were kind of my friends… So as a joke I said if you stop annoying me I'll give you a free boob squeeze. I thought they knew I was joking. They took it literally. They even told some other friends about it, I'd have random guys come up to me in the hall and touch my boobs. I know in a way its my fault, but I still feel violated by them.

I try and smile more these days. My boyfriends and I recently celebrated our one year. I know I should be happy, I know other people have it worse than me. But I'm still constantly tormented by the dark parts of my mind. My self harms gotten so much worse now… and I don't know what to do. My arms are covered in scars… they're getting harder to hide…

Please don't think badly of me for what I've told you… I know I've made mistakes in life, and I'm trying to do better, but it's hard when I feel like dying every day. Its hard to get better and recover when it's so easy to just pick up the blade. I just want you to know, I'm trying very hard to stay alive. I'm still in this fight: and I don't want to give up…

Chapter Fifteen — Julia

Hi,

Umm… I'm Julia, and I'm 16. I've actually started this letter a few times. I didn't know what to write about or how to explain myself. Welp, I hate myself every thing about myself. I'm too fat, I'm not smart enough. I'm not good at anything, but screwing up. You don't seem to mind people's stories and I've never told my whole story before so… here goes nothing. July 13th 1996 a girl was born after 2 days of labor and ending with a c-section. At this time her parents an her lived in New York. Her father was able to support the three of them fairly well. Until her brother was born.

Mom and Dad both had to work and this meant moving to Florida. Julia was five years old. Grade K was fine as every five year old deserves to be happy. 1st was okay. 2nd her little sister was born not long before Christmas. Then was the accident. The accident that started a chain reaction that changed everything. My dad drove tractor trailors, he was a truck driver. One day the person who loaded his truck did it wrong. He was going to unload it, and every thing inside of it fell on him. Today it was bank safes that he was transporting. There were three that really screwed him up. He was always in pain, and with what happened he should have been paralyzed.

After this he tried to work for most of third grade. There was the one really big fight that I walked on to when my dad threw the peanut butter and jelly jars across the kitchen. Other than that our year was fairly good. Fourth grade… started off okay. In my school the Tuesday before Thanksgiving we had Grandparents day. And being in fourth grade on Grandparents' Day meant you got to be in the play. My dad promised he would video tape it. He didn't. He had ODed the night before. It's so scary being nine years old and seeing your father who only seems to be asleep being carried away on a stretcher one day before Thanksgiving.

He was in the hospital for two months. Nobody told me anything so of course I asume I did everything wrong and got all As for the rest of the year. I just wanted them to stop fighting. They didn't. Dad moved out mom filed for divorce. In fifth grade a boy told me I was fat and ugly. Great self confidence booster. The Summer after I decided I wanted to be tiny so I ate every other day, and binged every other day. Sixth grade was the most stable year except for the fact I had no friends. That summer was the first time I wanted to really die, and I would have. 4 bottles of Advil. 20 tylenol.

My mom's current boyfriend had made me feel like I should die. I wanted nothing more than to show him how low he made me feel. To bad my mom noticed how hurt I was, and made me spend the night with her. The next night was the first time I cut. Then was seventh grade when my life was looking up mom was going to A.A.

She was single but a bitch without her morning vodka and evening rum. In October my dad was getting sick again. Nobody would notice that didn't live with him. Thank God I only lived with him every other weekend and Wendesdays. He started smoking more and more pot and taking more and more painkillers. He was falling more and more and sometimes I would have to go outside put out his half-smoke joint, and attempt to drag him inside. My sister had just turned 5 and my brother was 7 I was 12 and it was December 31st at 8:20 A.M. my father was pronounced dead. He had over dosed on the 28th. My siblings didn't know until the 2nd.

I remember everyone wanted me to make all these decisions, but nobody would let me do anything. My mom wasn't allowed to do anything as their divorce had been completed not long before. For about 9 months I lied about how hurt and sad I was. I threw myself into school work tried out for cheerleading and decided I was going to be skinny. 8th grade was the year I was a cheerleader it was a girl on the cheer team with me who taught me about total self destruction. She introduced me to "naughty" social networking sites. She taught me then set me loose.

I was 13. I was cutting every night, taking naked pictures every night, staying up till 3AM having phone sex. My mom thought I was on drugs. Then cheerleading ended. My dad was still dead. I was still ugly. But hey I had random guys all random ages telling me how beautiful I was if I took pictures for them. February my mom noticed my arms and noticed how sad I was. She took away my phone and promised if she ever saw another cut she would make me live with my grandparents. I stopped for a while.

Freshman year Thanksgiving morning, my mom and I got in the worst fight ever. We were on our way to morning Mass and she made me get out and walk home. I got home went to the medicine cabinet and took everything I could find. Around 4 o'clock that day I couldn't breath, they made me go to the hospital, they asked me what I did. I was sent in to a 72 hour lock down

at the mental hospital. I didn't eat nor sleep, and I told them what they wanted to hear. The doctor told me to think more clearly. I shook it all off went back to school. My mom punished me for wanting to die. She took away computer and phone again. In March she told me I could switch schools. My best friend and I switched together. I was clean from everything till December. December I met this boy who introduced me to Mary Jane. I stopped going to school. Then for Christmas I got a laptop, and before to long I was back to 8th grade, but worse.

That boy would make me feel like an ugly nothing. So I went online and online boys were so much nicer if you were nice to them. I was on webcam doing things that made me feel like nothing but at least I was pretty. That's what they said. What they promised. But my grades fell fast and I was always high then my grandma died and I had to be strong for everyone to replace what my dad couldn't do because he's dead. I was crying myself to sleep I was cutting. I wanted to die. Over the summer I got my act together then there was the bus accident. July 13th my 16th birthday I was in a church bus driving to Atlanta Georgia. 10 seconds we side-swiped a horse trailer with all of our stuff in it. I got the worst of it. Nicked my left arm artery, glass in my muscles, and I was scared that 8 year old I had in my lap was hurt.

Out of everything I had never been so scared. My mom home in Florida. Nobody knew if I was going to be okay. My "friends" when I got home were laughing like it was a joke. I started cutting again. I have been cutting. I do cry myself to sleep every night. There has been nothing "naughty" from me since the accident. I just wish it had killed me. Now here I am sitting in math class and it took me 4 days to write this letter.

I'm giving you my story and my razors . Thank you so much.

Julia

Chapter Sixteen — "K"

Hi,

I don't really know if you will read this or not, but if you happen to I just want to say thank you… thank you for posting a video that I had come across on tumblr and made me feel so inspired to let go of this object that had helped bring the pain to my skin. I know by sending away this object that holds so many dark memories I can now begin to let go and move on. I won't be able to harm myself anymore. I hope you know, you are helping a person and many others too that need somewhere to begin cleaning up their lives. It may be the first or the last time but this has helped majorly and I'm looking forward to a healthy future.

Thanks again,

K

Chapter Seventeen — Kaitlyn

July 20, 2:46 am

Dear Elijah,

My name is Kaitlyn, I'm 14 years old; and I want to share my story with you. On July 27, 2007, I purged for the first time. I was 10 years old. I knew it was bad, so I promised myself I would never do it again. Three weeks later, I broke that promise. Shortly after that, I began cutting myself. I used whatever I could get my hands on, sometimes having to rely on my finger nails. My weight dropped drastically and for a 10 year old, I was extremely underweight. I tried to pull myself out of the pit that I was being pushed into, and made it out, for a while. I didn't self harm for a few months, I didn't purge for 3 months! In February of 2008, I started again, falling back into habits I thought I had broken. No one found out, I kept going. For two more years I continued hurting myself.

Then on December 18, 20120, I told my friend Stephanie, (a college age girl who went to my church) that I cut. She told me that if I didn't tell my mom, she would. I told my mom that night, she was furious, and put me in counseling with our pastor. This pastor did nothing to help me because he didn't understand.

I stopped until January 2011; where I picked up my bad habits again. By this time, my cuts were getting deeper, leaving scars. My parents made me join a swim team, which only resulted in teasing from the coaches and other swimmers, so I cut where they wouldn't see it; on my stomach. I kept going, until February 2nd, 2011. I was so fed up with everything I just wanted to die. At 3 am, crying, shaking, terrified, I wrote my suicide notes. One to my little brother, one to my parents, one to my best friend. I took 30 pain killers, laid down on the floor. I was 13 years old.

15 minutes later, I felt sick. I crawled to the bathroom, forced myself to throw up until I was dry heaving, and realizing that I didn't really want to die. I went on living my miserable life for another year, until January 2012. My very best friend told me she had been molested by her brother over 40 times, and that she also cut. I was devastated, and shortly after telling me, she told her parents, and on February 8, she was informed she would be spending the next 8 months in an impatient treatment facility, and that we would have no contact. I cried, and was heartbroken, at the thought of losing her for 8 months. The next day, I was feeling awful

about everything that was going on. I began searching my room for the blades I knew were hidden there. In the process of searching, I found a book titled "100 favorite Bible verses" I tossed it aside, but then picked it up and flipped through it for the first time. Philippians 4:13 "I can do all things through Christ who gives me strength." I began to cry, and realized for the first time in my life that there is a God who cares about me, who loves me, who died for me. I found all 86 blades hidden around my room, walked to the family room where my mom was reading and fell into her arms, giving her the blades, telling her everything the last 4 years had held, I told her I wanted help. I was put in counseling, soon after, I went to the doctor for a physical. I weighed in at 96 lbs, a very unhealthy weight for someone my height. That day, I was diagnosed with Bulimia, severe depression, and severe anxiety. There was talk of sending me to inpatient treatment, nutritionists, specialists. I was anemic, underweight, sad, unhealthy, and I regretted asking for help. I saw 2 nutritionist, an ED specialist, my regular doctor, and a therapist once a week for the first 3 months of treatment, and I still do.

I'm proud to say that I'm recovering with your help, God's help, and the support of my friends and family. On my birthday, July 24, it will be one month since I self-harmed and 3 weeks since I purged. (Big improvement considering a year ago, I was cutting 3-10 times a day and purging everything I ate.)

The time to recover is NOW. I've shared this testimony with two youth groups in the area as well as my tumblr and facebook. My goal is to help someone who is struggling like I am.

I guess the point of this letter is to tell you that there is hope. You may not see it now, you may not feel like it, but there is hope, and you will get through this battle.

Recovery isn't easy,

but it's worth it.

Kaitlyn

I can do all things through Christ who gives me strength. Philippians 4:13

Chapter Eighteen — Kaity

Elijah,

I don't even know how to start this letter. You're such an inspiration. Your story is truly amazing & you're wonderful. You should never feel sad. I know that isn't possible & it's not fair, but I'm not asking you to make it possible. I know you can't help it, but I can't stand to see someone as inspirational as you upset. It makes me sad.

You've helped me get through so much, whether you know it or not, Some of the times when you were on tinychat, I joined to have something to distract me from cutting. It always worked. When I'm sad I usually scroll through your blog for a while. You help so many people on a daily basis & I just want to say thank you. From them & from me, thank you.

I really wanted to send you my blades, to… but I couldn't. It was too hard. I promise you that I will though, so they will never hurt another person again. Eventually.

You deserve the best, so don't settle for anything other than that. By the way, good luck with Lauren. :D & if you don't get this package until after the fair thingy & the puzzle pieces & all that adorable stuff, I hope everything went well. :D

Sorry, I couldn't resist mentioning it. It's so adorable. Omg. I can't. sdklfjlak;j.

Okay, I'm transitioning back into my tumblr talk, it's 4:38am, & I'm tired. I really wanted this to be longer, but I have to go to the post office tomorrow & I need sleeeeeeep. Ugh.

Sorryyyy. I'll write you again sometime. :3

Remember, it's okay to stumble sometimes. It's okay to relapse. It's okay to say that you're not okay. You can be broken, as long as you promise to try & put the pieces back together. ♥

Bye!

Kaity

Alright, story time. :3

Erm, I've never really told my story before, so I don't exactly know how to start. I guess I'll start at what really caused my start on self-harm.

When I was six, my uncle molested me. He was the first person to ever say anything truly horrible to me, but he made it sound like a compliment. He told me I was lucky. Lucky that he was doing that to me, because there was no way anyone else ever would. He called me names & hit me. He was the first person to ever call my worthless. When I started crying he yelled more & said that sowing emotion was weak & that I shouldn't cry because it made me even uglier. I believed every word he said.

When I got home I was too embarrassed to say anything, so my family doesn't know. I don't think they ever will since we don't talk to my uncle anymore (for other reasons). You're actually one of the few people who know now.

Anyway, after that it just kinda went downhill. I started punching, biting, pinching, & anything else I could do to hurt myself because I thought I deserved it. I actually tried to break my arm once. If I hurt someone else, I hurt myself. If I did something wrong, I hurt myself.

Mistakes weren't allowed.

I felt dirty. Not physically, but in a way that I can't even describe. In a way where a million showers couldn't help. I felt like I wasn't good enough & like I didn't belong in my school, in my house, like I shouldn't even be alive. At the time I was eight years old. No one should ever be thinking about suicide, especially not when they're eight years old. It's quite sad, really. Since I was so young, the only thing I could do to try to end my life was attempt to drown myself in the bathtub, which obviously never worked out.

I'd like to say that I got better from there on, that the self-harm stopped, but it didn't. It got worse, actually. When I was twelve, I realized that I wanted, needed, more pain. The only way I could think of was cutting myself. I hadn't heard anything about it at that point, so I didn't know other people did it. I didn't know that it could & would become addicting. I was twelve, I didn't know anything about anything. But I did know that I wanted to hurt myself.

So I took a kitchen knife & I cut into my skin. I didn't know what to feel. It hurt a lot, but at the same time, it cleared my head. I hadn't been able to think clearly in a long time. Cutting felt like a breath of fresh air.

The cuts started as small scratches, barely even visible. Over time they got worse, a lot worse. The small scratches turned into cuts which turned into gashes which

Turned into gaping wounds that I had to keep bandaged for weeks before they healed.

Almost cutting to deep and barely staying alive became a habit. At the time, I didn't even care. People knew something was wrong. I wasn't eating, couldn't sleep, barely said a warod. Anyone with common sense would know something was wrong, but they didn't do anything about it.

My first real suicide attempt was earlier this year, towards the beginning of January. I don't really remember much of what happened, but I know that I simply walked upstairs, sad goodnight to my parents & told them I loved them, then I grabbed three bottles of pills from the bathroom.

I lined the pill up in a row on my desk, I was going to crush them up in a glass of water but I wanted a chance to back if I changed my mind. I turned on some music & I swallowed the first pill. In five minutes, I had swallowed half the row. There were tears streaming down my face & I was doing everything I could to concentrate on what I was supposed to be doing, ending my life. I had finished all the pills in ten minutes, and by that time I was getting dizzy & there were black spots in front of my eyes. I laid on my bed, closed my eyes, & everything went dark.

Then I woke up.

The next few days were a blur. All I know is that I was violently ill every time I tried to move. My parents wanted to take me to the Emergency Room but I convinced them that it was just food poisoning or the flu. I didn't know what went wrong, why I had woken up. I was supposed to be dead. I was supposed to be free. I was supposed to be free of the pain. I had killed my soul, but my body remained here to suffer.

I attempted two more times within the next six months, both obviously failing. It didn't even matter because I was already dead. I didn't need a gun, or a noose, or pills to tell me that. I had no personality, no friends, no motivation, I was nothing.

On August 2nd, 2012, I don't know what changed, I don't know what happened but I decided that I wasn't going to be a waste of space anymore. I started playing piano & violin again. I started to draw again, too. I was slowly becoming who I used to be.

I started the Butterfly Project, the Paper Chain Project, & even made recovery bracelets in hopes of recovering. I've relapsed a couple of times, but I'm determined to get better. I want to fix myself.

I might have scars on my arms, shoulders, stomach, thighs, & hips, but at least they're scars. & that's all they'll ever be now. They're a part of me that I'm proud to have because they symbolize a battle with myself that I've finally won. I do have moments of doubt, but everyone does. It's part of the process. I'm finally happy again, & I can say that without hesitation. There are a lot of people who have helped me along the way. Sadly, most of them don't live anywhere near me, but they've still managed to help more than anyone I know in real life. Most of them I actually met on Tumblr & we're really close now. They don't live in the same place as me, but I'm glad that I actually have people I can trust again. It's definitely helped a lot to know I have people to turn to when I want to relapse.

Even though I've struggled with cutting, depression, suicide, & and EDNOS (that's another long story, so I won't go into that), it's good to know that it does get better & everyone should be around to see that.

Chapter Nineteen — Katie

Dear Elijah,

I would like to tell you my story. Hi, my name is Katie. I'm 19 and I'm a dreamer. I have attempted suicide 12 times, but as of 10.15.12 I took a new realization of my life: I can't achieve my dreams if I'm dead.

(Left side: I HAVE CHEMICAL DEPRESSION)

My story: I AM BIPOLAR. It started when I was 12, 7th grade. I got called fat, ugly, a poser etc. It got to the point that I would cry myself to sleep every night. So I started to cut. Then after a month I stopped because I was a lead in the school musical, but I was still hurting so I took on the rubberband & just punching myself. I did that up until my freshman year. Attempted suicide: 6

That's when I started drinking my pain away. It didn't last long because people still called me ugly, fat, worthless. So I started starving myself. When people started questioning why I wasn't eating, I started eating but ended up throwing it all up. I was bullemic until the end of sophomore year. I finally had good friends that loved me.

I got my heart broken my sophomore & junior year so I started using the rubberband again, but I stopped when my BFF asked me too. Attempted suicide: 2

Now comes the sad part: My freshman year of college I was sexually harassed, almost raped, I was in so much pain so I started to cut again. I sat in my jakuzzi and cut so I could die. Someone ended showing up so I ended up leaving. Then the guy that harassed me stalked me for 2 weeks so I decided to take pills, but I ended up eating bad sushi so I threw it all up. I ended up quiting school and went back home. I live with my sister and I got an email from someone to just go kill myself□

so I took pills again, but I woke up. Then on july 23rd, 2012 I cut again to die. I'm obviously still alive. I am getting better slowly but surely. Attempted suicide: 4

Your videos are so hauntingly BEAUTIFUL.

I'm staying alive because of One Direction, on one of my suicide attempts what makes you beautiful played so I am alive because of them. My dream is to meet them. My biggest dream though is to be a singer. I have videos on youtube & I am trying out for the x-Factor.

I just want to say thank you for caring. It's because of you I am fighting for my dreams & my life. Thank you!

Katie

Chapter Twenty — Meg

Dear Elijah! (It's meg)

I'm writing you this letter because I didn't know how else to thank you, I know its not much but I cant afford to send you a big package from England.

Ok so this might sound cliché but you really are amazing, you have been threw stuff that no one should have to go threw and you have come out a better person, you really are so strong.

I'm sorry that I can not even make you a bracelet. I think you have enough, and Im shit at that sort of thing anyway, I'm not really any good at anything.

Well I'm sure I have probably been really annoying you on twitter, but I have told you things that I haven't ever told anyone else, and if you think I'm being stupid or whatever, but I just, I can't change the way I feel about myself, you can tell me I'm beautiful, or that I deserve happiness, but it doesn't change the fact that everyday I will be told I'm ugly and fat, that I'm worthless and all the rest of it.

I am meant to be doing my college work as I have 5 essays to do, but I decided you are more important. I have never met anyone who cares about other people as much as you do!

I'm sorry that I'm not strong enough to send you my blades because without them I wouldn't be able to stay here, and I can't send you my suicide letter because I might need it, because I'm really not strong. However, if I do get threw this, when I have a baby I will name him or her Elijah, becaure you're the one who tried to help me, your the one who told me I was good enough, and I know I don't believe you, but I am thankfull, I really am. I know that this is just a stupid letter from a girl who has shit hand writing and cant spell but, I wanted to say thankyou, and not just on twitter or tumblr. Elijah I am so so proud of you, you have come so far, and you are so strong. To be honest without you I would be dead right now. I know you said you didn't want me to be the person you couldn't save and I no I just a second said I wouldn't, but I will send you my suicide letter because I want to get better for you. I can't send you my blades because they are what help me stay alive, I will stop smoking for you though, if you want me to. I will send you my story, it is not very special or anything , but if you want it I can send it to you.

In all your video's you say "I'm sorry" and it breaks my heart to see you get upset because you can't help everyone. People send you there blades, I need you to make sure you do not get trigged and that they really don't ever hurt anyone agian.

You told me that other people broke my brain but I don't think they did, I can't blame other people for my issues. It is my own fault I cut, it's my fault I'm ugly and fat. I'm disgusting and that's just the truth.

Because I'm shit at everything I have this picture with your quote on I Dunno why.

Even though I'm sending you my suicide letter I can not promise you I won't write another one but I'm going to try.□

If your reading this its probably to late, I probably really did it. I'm sorry everyone, I really am, I just couldn't do it anymore, please nobody blame yourself, it's not your fault. I'm so so sorry I just couldn't do it anymore. I don't talk to anyone or tell you how I feel I'm sorry. I'm not gunna write an 8 page long thing explaining, because because it doesn't matter, it's not important, I'm gone now and I won't be coming back. I will be looking down on you all, forever. I am so sorry I did this, I don't no what else to say. You can carry on with your life like it was before, just without me, I'm so sorry everyone. I just can't do this any more Im not strong enough, it all hurts to much and its not getting better. Nobody cry, please, Im not worth your tears.

Im so sorry. I love you all.

Love from, Megan

xxxx

PS: goodbye, sorry

PPS: You cant hurt me anymore, because I did this to myself

Oh please wear pink to my funeral? It would mean alot! Xxx

Chapter Twenty One — Parris

Hi Elijah, I hope your having a great day. □ I apologize in advance if I spell things wrong, I'm not the greatest speller. My name is Parris and I'm a huge fan of yours, I've watched all your videos & I check your tumblr about everyday. I sent you a few messages on tumblr, but you never replied. I'm sorry for sending them, cuz I didn't realize how many you get, the other day you said you had about 5,000. I figured sending an actual piece of mail would be less bothersome, for you get less mail that way.

You inspire me, you really do, not because your overcoming your struggle but because of how you are. You made a blog it got popular & people began to ask you for help, and you don't get mad and be like read my FAQ are you fuckin stupid, no you actually try to help them, even though its not your job. And I know I don't know you, I've only come to a conclusion of how you are from your blog & your videos, so if I'm totally wrong or come off as rude, I'm sorry.

This is going to address some of the points in your past, with a picture of you (which I think looks good cuz I think you have really pretty eyes), and it starts with 'This is going to be a selfish post where I talk about myself' (which its not 'selfish' cuz its your blog, and you can post whatever the you want) That's another thing, I tend to write how I speak, and when I speak I tend to swear alot, so I'm sorry if it comes off wrong or you take offense.

Anyways you don't look awful, agian you have really pretty eyes, and iono if your sick or just feel bad or sad, it doesn't matter I hope you feel better. I'm sure you'll finish with Laurens gift and even if you don't she seems like the type of person who could truley appreciate the effort you put into it. (I stalk her blog as well, and I think you've got a good one there, don't let that go) I don't know why you haven't been to work, but that's ok, just relax and don't stress it, it'll all be fine.

I really hope that you were able to fight the self-harm urges, and if you did end up self-harming, its ok, you're still a beautiful human being and you can come back from it. I couldn't imagine trying to fight it with people sending blades, that's another reason I find you soo inspirational, is even with that you still want people to send them to you, you want to help them.

I don't know how you handle the urges or cont'd it, but the strange thing I do is I take a tak and I kinda chew on the plastic side where the metal pokey part isn't in your mouth or isn't poking you or anything, and iono, I know its pretty weird, but it kinda makes me feel confortable or safe, I'm not really sure how to explain it, but because its there I don't' really get those urges as much. Iono I was just thinkin that might help you a bit.

Even if you don't want to eat, you should anyway, cuz I figure your just like ehhh food, but just eat some stuff anyway. Nobody knows what to do all the time, and not knowing is ok, you'll figure it out eventually. I think your really stressing or sort of panicky about the fact you don't know what to do, for you put it 3 times.

And again I can't stress enough how OK it is to not know, knowing ins't important, just do what you feel is right. I don't know all that's happening in your life right now, but I think maybe your need to help people is a factor to why your depression may be coming back. I think in your head you've set a bar for yourself, that's really high maybe because people keep telling you that you are so great and inspirational and help them so much, they trust you, and go to you for help.

So you feel like your task is the help people, but so many people come to you, its not possible to help so many people. And knowing that these people, come to you, some with thier lives, you try your best to help & do what you can, but your only one person. You can't help everyone, and I think that's wats starting to get to you. Just know that helping just one person is something to be proud of. You impact peoples lives in a positive way and that's something to be proud of.

Theres not this huge expectation of you, people you actually know, and your followers are aware you have your own shit to deal with, you don't live for us, you need to take care of yourself & the ones closest to you first. Would like to be able to take care of everyone, sure, but you can't. It's not that we (people of the internet, your followers & whatnot) are putting the expectation on you that you're an inspirational blog/help blog, its not that we see your blog that way, its how we see you.

You inspire people, because of your genuine wanting to help people, for some reason it seems so pure hearted, and your ability to do that/feel that way, and still struggle, that is what is inspiring to people. Because you've struggled/ing & are overcoming it, makes people feel as if you get it, you understand what they are feeling & can help them, in addition they feel that pure hearted want/need to help, that is why people come to you for help.

You follow is the advice of your heros/icons right? Well some people see you as such, & want the advice of their hero; Elijah. Another reason people come to you is you seem like you don't judge, and no one wants to feel like they are being judged, its one of the worst feelings in the world. I know that your prolly kinda scared to have shit coming back, and maybe feeling a bit helpless cuz you don't think be there for people and your letting everyone down. It's fuckin OK, your not letting anyone down, i think everyone knows your doing the best you can.

And the little things you do for people, they matter alot, what you do, more like, how you are is appreciated. No one ever seems ok, because no one is, everyone struggles with something no matter how big or how small. If your really set on speaking at a school, you might be able to speak at mine, though I love far from you. I go to (omitted) Highschool, (omitted) the number is (omitted) and the address is (omitted).

Iono how to go about any of that, but if you want theres the information. If you happen to need to talk, there's so many people that care about you, who would love to talk to you and care about you, such as your girlfriend, but if you end up needing someone, I'm here. You are an amazing and beautiful human being, have a great day, and a long wonderful life. Oh & I'm really sorry its so long or if you hate it or if this was bother some or annoying or you somehow get offended. I'm sorry & yeah.

To end on a light and humeros note:

Mother mother fuck. Mother mother fuck fuck. Mother fuck mother fuck.

Noise Noise Noise.

One Two

One Two Three four

Noise noise noise

Smokin weed, smokin weed

Drink beers, beers, beers

Rollin fatties, smoking blunts

Who smokes the blunts? We smoked the blunts

Rollin blunts & smoking uh

15 buds little man, put that shit in my hand, if that money doesn't show you owe me, owe me, owe me, oh, my jungle love, oh ee, ohee, oh ee, oh

- If you get it great, if not it's the song they are singing in the beginning of Jay & Silent Bob Strike Back, one of Kevin Smith's movies, it's like my favorite, along with his others Chasing Amy, Mallrats, Dogma, Clerks, & Clerks 2. I love Kevin Smith, especially with Jason Mewes, they are just so perfect.

Ok, rambling sorry, again have a fabulous day & a long, beautiful, joyful, funfilled life. □

Oh, and I just realized I was spost to write something about me or my story. Well I havn't really got a story, I'm boring, all I really do is sit in my room when I get home from school. I watch way to much tv. I'm 15 and I'm going to be 16 in December, I'm currently in 10th grade. I'm somewhat fucked up in the brain. Not in like a physchopath way, but I do self harm and whatnot, its not that bad, none of my cuts are really that deep.

I don't have many friends, but the ones I have I cherish & love dearly, for I'm lucky to have them. I'm not the most likable person in the world, I'm mean, heartles, and never do anything for others, or so I've been told. Though I try to help everyone, I fail, alot of people will end up just getting mad at me, and all my friends get bored & leave sooner or later as well. That's ok though, cuz I get it, and they deserve a better friend then I can be, I expect it but it still hurts when it actually happens. I will go out of my way for people, but it doesn't seem to matter.

Even with all my efforts I'm aware that I'm still not doing anything to help or for them at all, I do it for myself so I don't feel so bad. I'm way too big, I weight over 200 pounds, & no matter what I do It won't go away, and its driving me insane, every time I look in the mirror I just want to cry, especially if I take my make up off. I just really try to avoid mirrors, and scales. And I love to go shopping but I hate it at the same time cuz the stuff I like, I can't find in my size & it makes me want to just cry.

I don't bother people I know abouts any of it, because I know its stupid and would prolly just be bothersome & annoying for them, and they would prolly leave soon if they knew. I don't look like one to struggle. If you knew me and saw how I carry myself around people, you wouldn't think anything was ever wrong with me either. I'm not as bad as other people, so I really don't think it's a problem, cuz other people have actual reasons to feel this way and I just kinda do.

It started when I moved from where I had such amazing friends & was just so happy to a place where no one would ever fuckin talk to me & I'd hear them makin fun of me. I moved from there 6 months later, and now I'm here, its alot better than Big Bear but I can't shake the feeling that being there gave me. I'm also not as bad as others cuz im not really suicidal. I say not really, cuz I want to die but I can't do it, I'm too weak, it more of if I happened to get hit by a car, I wouldn't care.

I always walk on the street side, you knw when you're walking with people and theres the person on the end, where if a car were to come it would hit them that's where I walk at, I always move people to the inside so if one comes it would hit me instead of them. Well I'm sorry if this was just annoying or bothersome, but ya. Again have a wonderful day and don't forget that you truly are a glowing, beautiful, amazing human being.

Chapter Twenty Two — "RLA"

Elijah,

I'm mailing you to let you know you inspire me. You inspire lots of people but there's a specific reason why you inspire me. You've dedicated your life to reaching out to others. I'll be the first to tell you that it is a bittersweet thing. While you have gone through your own struggles and come out with a new perspective, there will always be a piece of your mind stuck in that old life. To heal others when you're in a perpetual healing state? That's bloody heroic. So while you give us a challenge, I give you a challenge: take every letter I send to hear and decide how you'll use it to continue healing. I found you on Tumblr so hopefully I'll know if you decide to take my challenge as seriously as I take yours.

-RLA

Chapter Twenty Three — Sam

Dear Elijah,

Your videos are amazing. They give me hope that I can live another day.

My name is Sam. I'm fifteen years old. However, things are not as… Good? As one would wish. I have been cutting myself since I was twelve. I have attempted suicide six times the past two years or so. Mainly because of abuse from an ex-boyfriend, self-hatred, verbal abuse from peers, those kinds of things. I honestly don't know why I'm writing this letter. I guess I thought you might understand.

Lately, my depression has gotten worse for no reason. My cutting got worse, my suicidal thoughts worsened as well. But I stumbled across your blog on tumblr. Your self harm video got to me. I want to stop cutting, but I don't want to. I'm afraid of relapse because each relapse is worse than the last. I don't know what to do. It's as if I've become a slave to it, yet I'm afraid to leave it.

Anyway, if you read this, it was just saying thank you. Your videos kept me from attempting again. So… Thank you.

Best Regards,

Sam

Chapter Twenty Four – Sammi

September 15, 2012

Dear Elijah,

So today while scrolling through tumblr. I saw an instead of cutting post. Instead of cutting #781 Watch justaskinnyboy on YouTube. 25 minutes later, here I am, sitting on my bed at 10:20 pm writing you this letter.

I'm sixteen years old and I'm a junior in high school. Quite honestly, it's a frickin' miracle that I made it this far. My parents divorced when I was three because my father is a raging alcoholic (who will be getting married for the fifth time in October) and was abusive. My mom and I move(d) every two-three years so I don't have friendships that have been since first grade. Nada. My grandpa, my best friend, died six years ago, less than a month before my birthday. Smiles on my birthday? No. Tears. Since then I have developed severe depression, have self-harmed and have attempted suicide multiple times.

I was able to keep my cutting a secret until last year I finally broke down and told my two best friends who then used force to drag me into our guidance counselor's office. After showing the counselor my wrist, she told my mother. My mother's reaction? Screaming when I asked to see an outside-of-school counselor and only speaking to me when absolutely necessary. It's a really good thing she found out in November because I was allowed to use a disposable razor until February. Thank God for electric razors. But when she fought me by taking the razors, I walked to the drug store on Main Street and bought a bag. I can now dismantle a disposable razor in under 3 minutes. The cuts started getting longer, deeper and fewer days were in between when I would do it.

I've been seeing a therapist every other week for almost a year now and I was eight months clean before relapsing *applause for me* Dude omg! I forgot! My name is Sam. Kcool. My mom is always so interested in what I talk about during my sessions, but never about why I do what I do. It almost makes me feel like she doesn't care.

I have three really awesome friends that I've told my story to: Jake, Jess, Ramon. Jake's known the longest. He's helped me find a more positive way to deal with my emotions, but it only works sometimes. I made a wall of mini drawings/doodles that are positive. Jess has had multiple friends commit suicide so when I get those feelings I call her, or I write my letter and give it to her the next day. Ramon is the easiest to talk to because I tell him absolutely everything that goes on in my head. Today I asked him if school buses have penises. I actually just got off of the phone with him because thinking about all of this is a huge trigger. The worst part is the best way I know to keep from crying is to cut. Vicious cycle I know.

There's more.

"July 24, 2012

Dear journal,

So now I'm ready to fucking kill myself. I feel judged and misunderstood. I feel alone and helpless. I feel lost. I can't do this. I can't live like this for the rest of my life. With the state/mood I'm in tonight I'll be lucky if I make it to Saturday without cutting myself. Are we having fun yet?

- S"

I feel like that all the time and I absolutely hate it. Your videos make me feel like there is hope. I wish I could put into words how much I needed that today.

I'm enclosing my latest suicide note because it has been sitting on my nightstand. Waiting. I'm also putting two of my blades in here. It's a start… there are more but now I have less (if that made sense) but wait! There's more. The square picture I keep over my bed on my ceiling right about my posted that I made that says "Love is louder than the pressure to be perfect." The other two are from my inspiration wall. I wasn't you to have them as a reminder of how much you've inspired me to recover.

Thank you so much. I love you.

-Sammi

Wait! Thank you for taking the time to read this. And if it's not too much to ask, could you mail me a replay letter?

I'm doing this because I don't know what else to do. I'm trapped, slowly suffocating. If you're analyzing or trying to remember the last conversation we had, stop. Don't stress yourself over it. I can guarantee that this wasn't your fault and I'm sorry that you have to deal with this but it's sort of too late to do anything, or at least it will be by the time you read this.

I suppose this is when I would say I'm sorry. But funny story, I'm really not. I needed to do this for myself. And if you don't agree with me decision. I don't care. Didn't when I was alive and still don't now that I killed myself. Yup. I said it. I committed suicide. I offed myself. Gave up. I always thought that writing this note, like for real, would be hard. That I wouldn't know where to begin and I would be crying so hard you wouldn't be able to even read the whole letter. That's why I practiced on the sides of my notes all last year. I did it in class so that I would have no choice but to suppress my emotions. Pretty smart if I do say so myself.

So this is it.

Bye.

-S

Chapter Twenty Five – Stacey

My name is Stacey, I'm 18, and I'm a college freshman. I've spent the past six years dealing with major depression, self harm issues, anxiety, and "food issues". I know that you say you are nothing special, but in a sense, you are. I'm probably giving you too much credit, but, today, today you are saving my life.

Last month, I tripped. I gave in, and it got so bad that I was contemplating taking my own life. It's hard, getting back up after six years of failure. It gets harder every time I try again, because I'm so used to failing, so I stopped believing in myself. It's hard living in a house parents say I just need to grow up, who don't listen, who won't even try to understand. When you're living in a world full of unforgiving faces, and when you are dealt one shitty situation after another, it becomes hard to even think about being happy again.

I'm not going to spill my story to you, I don't think it's right, putting that on you. But, your words, truly keep me going. I'll wake up in a dark place, and I'll just load one of your videos for some kind words, so I can actually get out of bed that day. Some days are harder than others, but knowing that someone out there understands, makes it a little easier.

So, today, everything changes. I am reaching out to anyone who will listen. I am taking the first step, for the billionth time, and I am trying to see things in a different perspective. You know, I didn't think I was ever going able to say that, that I am going to try again. But you, and your words, and your messages, has given me a new hope. Seeing you, still trying to get better, gives me a little strength, because if you can do it, then so can I.

Elijah, thank you. I am taking the first step. I want to get better, so take them, the blades, that have hurt me countless times, tiny as they may be, they have left scars that will never fade, caused pain I thought I deserved for things I couldn't control. I don't need them anymore. I'm not saying that I will never hurt myself again, but this is the first step in order to get there, because I deserve better than this.

I'll end up writing again,
probably to give an update,
even if you don't remember me,

it would be nice to let you know.
Thank you so much, Elijah.
I wish you all the best, because you deserve happiness.

Stay strong..

So I've been wanting to tell someone my story for awhile, but I've just been too scared. But I need to tell my story, I need to tell someone before it kills me. So, here it goes. It might be a little jumpy, but I'm just typing as I remember things.

I was 12, when he raped me. 12. In that moment I was forced to grow up.

I never told anyone what happened, and I really haven't until now. It's been six years, and I still feel that twang of pain when I'm remember what happened. I still blame myself on a daily basis. Even though I know it wasn't my fault, I still blame myself.

My self-hate...along with the low self-esteem...made me sink...into this pit. I quickly became depressed.

I was 13 when I put a blade to my wrist. Never deep enough for stiches, just deep enough to feel the pain. It was my punishment, for everything. Got a bad grade? Cut. Got yelled at? Cut. Didn't live up to my friends/parents expectations? Cut.

I was 14 when high school started. I didn't really have any friends, and I wouldn't really let myself open up to anyone. I was lumped in as an outcast, an emo, a freak. Cutting wasn't punishment anymore. It was the only way I could feel anything, because feeling pain was better than feeling nothing.

I was 15, straight A student, still depressed, still harming myself, it was at that point, when people started to say "Hey, have you gained weight?" I became super self-conscious about my weight, and my eating habits have been poor ever since.

I was 16, straight B student, a couple friends who knew my secrets, but I could never really let anyone in.

I was 17, a C or D student, even in my honors classes; my best friend was in a coma, a close family friend died. A couple close friend's tried to kill themselves. I was made fun of for my scars, for being different. I was in the counselor's office on and off for that entire year, not willingly, but because I was reported by friends who were worried I was going to hurt myself.

Along with the depression, and the self-harm, and other issues, I also sleep. I was exhausted, but I physically could not sleep, and when I did it was because I would collapse from exhaustion. My sleeping is still so unpredictable, I can go for days on nothing but a couple hours, or I can sleep for 12+ at a time.

I was getting worse, and worse, and no one even noticed. I would lock myself in my room for days...crying, sleeping, staring at the wall. I ignored everyone and everything, my friends abandoned me. I had completely secluded myself from the world.

I would shred my skin until there was nowhere left to cut. I was numb anyway, it's not like it mattered. I would stand in front of my mirror, pulling at my skin, at my fat, hoping it would go away. I wasn't good enough for anyone..

When I would leave my room, I would be yelled at. I was a bitch, or fat, worthless, ugly, a failure, a disappointment, the problem child. What kind of parents would call their daughter names? Mine, they never tried to understand. They didn't want to acknowledge that something else was wrong with me. They refused to see what was wrong. Even when school would call home worried, they just turned the other way. It hurts knowing that they didn't even care enough to help me. They still tell me to "grow up" and "get over it, your not sad, just be happy." It's crazy, that everyone else in my family has a mental disorder, but it's not ok for me to not be ok.

During this, I had been dating someone for about 4 years. He would always poke at me, and tell me how "squishy" I was (like I wasn't worried about my weight enough), he never resorted to calling me fat, but the thought was always there. Even though he had depression and self harmed, he would always make fun of me for it. "hey what are those? Oh fresh cuts, your such a freak" "Oh what..you 'depression' is really bad today, so?" When he did get tired of me, he would leave, and I would beg him to come back. He would, but only if he had no one else to screw with. Eventually, he convinced me that I didn't need anyone else but him, that he could save me, and that I would never find anyone else. I eventually lost all of my friends, and I ended up only having him. He wasn't always a horrible person, but it was all the bad times that still stand out.

I never really knew how emotionally abusive, or what he had done to me, until he finally decided he was done with me. We had gotten engaged, and then he cheated on me, and basically said I was nothing to him. He said that she was better, and smarter, and she loved him more, and that she was "normal".

After he left, he took my oxygen with me. I had no one, and didn't want to live anymore, and in February of 2012 I tried to kill myself. Amazingly, I woke up, in my own bed...I hadn't done enough. . .I've never told anyone..

Even though I almost failed senior year, I miraculously made it through high school. I thought, that everything was going to be better..

Seven months of recovery happened after my attempt, but at the beginning of August, I slipped again...

I don't really know what happened..everything just got so out of control, my life went to hell, and I had no control over it.

I had to quit my dream college, because I just was so afraid of what I might do to myself, I was afraid of everything.

Anxiety ran rampant, my depression got worse..there are more scars..but I got back up.. determined to fight again...

Only a month later, I relapsed, hard.

At the beginning of September, the man that ruined my life came back into town, and all of the memories came rushing back.

No eating, no sleeping, I left more scars on my body, they'll never fade away.

I discovered you shortly after he came back. I wrote you a letter, and sent you my blades, and said that I was better than self harm. Some nights, when I'm on the edge, I just listen to your videos for words of wisdom.

I acquired more blades half way through November, and I must admit that I have used them, but I have been working up the courage to send them to you, and I guess today I am. All of them, every, single, one. And this time I am promising you that I will never hurt myself again.

It's amazing, that in the past six years, I've never been hospitalized, I've never been sent to treatment. I saw a psychologist up until right after I was diagnosed with depression and anxiety, but then stopped seeing them, because my mother stopped believing me, and therapy. I was on medication for a short time, but I haven't been in years.

I'm 18, a third of my life has been hell. It still is, and every day is a constant struggle between life and death. It always will be. But I'm trying.

I have recently connected with an old friend from high school. He graduated the year before I did, and we lost touch. We are actually dating now :) He is surprisingly understanding, but I guess that's due to the fact that we share the same disorders, we support each other. It's the best feeling, knowing that after everything, there's still someone out there who won't leave, but I guess you know about that.

I haven't stood up to my mother yet, her verbal and emotional abuse still brings me to tears on a daily basis, but I'm hoping to move out with a friend later this year.

I also went back to college, and I'm working on my nursing degree.

The world is full of darkness; it's hard to forget the bad things that happen in the past, but in order to move forward, you have to forget, no matter how difficult.

I've met some amazing people in the past few months, I have a new support system. I really hope to meet them all one day.

I have no regrets, you would think that I would, but I don't. Everything that that has happened has made me who I am today. My story isn't over yet, it's a work in progress, I have recently been given the opportunity to move forward. I'm not going to stop this time. I'm not going to look back. It's time for me to be happy. **It's time for me to beat this.**

Index of Topics

Special Thanks To:

Rebecca M.

~

Jacob & Jennifer Beasley

~

Ian A. Chapman

Thank you for believing in this project and for supporting us in making this book a reality!

Made in the USA
Middletown, DE
01 October 2015